Philadelphia Bird Food Company

The Bird Food Company's Book of Cage Birds

Philadelphia Bird Food Company

The Bird Food Company's Book of Cage Birds

ISBN/EAN: 9783744646437

Printed in Europe, USA, Canada, Australia, Japan

Cover: Foto ©Andreas Hilbeck / pixelio.de

More available books at **www.hansebooks.com**

THE BIRD FOOD COMPANY'S

BOOK OF

CAGE BIRDS:

Their Diseases and Remedies; with Instructions for Breeding and keeping them in constant Health and Song.

THE PHILADELPHIA
BIRD FOOD COMPANY,
NO. 400 NORTH THIRD STREET,
PHILADELPHIA.
1894.

SEED-EATING BIRDS.

To this class belong all birds that live exclusively on seeds. Different species require different seed, but the general management is the same. Canary seed forms the staple diet of nearly all varieties, and is grown principally in Egypt, Turkey, Sicily, and Spain. It is of as many grades and qualities as wheat, and here arises the reason of the non-success of most people with cage birds. They go to an apothecary shop, a grocery store, or a bird establishment, and ask for canary seed. Without examination they take what is given them; which, in nine cases out of ten, is Smyrna, a variety of canary seed that is as hard and almost as indigestible as flint; is full of dust, and seeds of injurious weeds; and is often old and rancid. Consequently, the bird soon becomes dull, breathes with difficulty, and lingers on for months a songless ball of feathers, until finally death ends its miserable existence.

The only canary seed that should be given to a bird is that grown in Spain and Sicily. It is larger and of brighter color than the inferior grades, and is easily cracked. Even this must be selected with much care, as sometimes on the journey across the Atlantic the bags get wet with salt water and the seed becomes worthless; as it also does if not properly cleansed from dust; or when more than a year old.

The package seed with which the country is flooded consists of Smyrna canary seed or the cheap grades of Spanish, mixed with American rape and millet seed, and is sure death to birds fed upon it for a length of time. The seed sold at most bird stores is no better. Many of the brands contain hemp seed, which is very injurious to canaries and many other varieties of cage birds, and should be fed but sparingly to all species; for being very fattening and heating, it ruins the digestive organs and spoils the voice; moreover all seed-eating birds are inordinately fond of this seductive poison and will scarcely eat any other seed as long as they can get hemp.

We have made the proper diet and care of cage birds a life-study and our package goods, it is believed, contain the only correct foods for all species of birds, that have ever been placed on the American market.

Our *Mixed Seed* consists of a combination of seeds that is best adapted to nearly all species of seed-eating birds. The mixture is: four parts, best quality Sicily canary, carefully cleaned and selected, and always the crop of the current year; three parts, sweet German summer rape; two parts, India millet; and one part, Turkish maw seed. It can be had at almost every first-class drug store throughout the United States. The price is 10 cents for pint, and 20 cents for quart packages. Be sure to see that the label is the same as shown in the engraving, and as you value the life and song of your birds accept no substitute.

We can deliver one pint of our best Mixed Seed or of plain Sicily Canary Seed by mail to any P. O. in the U. S. for 15c.

We also put up the *Sicily Canary Seed* in the same size packages as the Mixed Seed; it is sold at the same prices.

All birds need gravel strewn on the bottom of the cage daily, or every other day at the longest.

Either *Red* or *Silver Gravel* may be used but we advise the former, as birds are very fond of it, and it helps to digest the food. Silver Gravel, although cleaner in the cage, is not eaten so readily; while, being sharp and glass-like in its nature, sometimes causes the death of the bird that swallows it, by cutting through the craw.

We box both kinds, the price for each being 10 cents for the quart, and 5 cents for the pint size. The postage on one pint of gravel is 30 cents, so that our price when sent by mail is 35 cents per pint.

A piece of Cuttle-Fish Bone should be kept constantly

in the cage of all seed-eating birds, as they sharpen their bills upon it and also occasionally eat it, and being slightly salt in its nature, it is very beneficial. Every owner of a bird knows what a troublesome thing it is to keep a cuttlebone between the bars of a cage, and that the holders that are sold are very unsatisfactory fastenings. We have patented a combined cuttle bone and holder, the simplicity of which is shown by the engraving. The entire surface of the bone is accessible to the bird, and it is held firmly in position until every particle of friable matter is gone. It is sold at 5 cents for a fine selected bone and holder, and it can be had of druggists, or will be mailed on receipt of price.

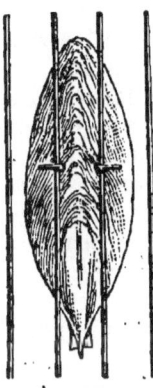

The canary breeders of the Hartz Mountains of Germany use a paste to keep their birds in constant health and song, and to cure nearly all diseases, the ingredients of which are a secret to all but a few of the peasants. Recently we came into possession of the recipe, and now manufacture the paste, having christened it "Bird Manna." It is put up in a little metal case (secured by *letters patent*), which fasten to the cage wires within reach of the bird. It has been thorouhgly tested for over ten years, and we have received thousands of testimonials of its curing all diseases that cage birds are subject to, and causing birds to sing that were silent for a long period

BIRD MANNA.

Showing both sides.

If given to a bird during the season of shedding feathers, it will in most cases carry the little musician through this critical period without loss of song. If used according to directions, one Manna will last a bird many weeks. It can be had of druggists or will be sent by mail for 15 cents.

SOFT-BILLED BIRDS.

To this class belong all birds that live on a varied diet of seeds, berries, and insects. They are more delicate in confinement than seed-eating birds, but are finer and sweeter songsters, and well repay the extra care and trouble.

Their diet should consist principally of Prepared Mocking Bird Food, but care should be taken to see that only our food is used, nearly all other being cheaply made and not fit for birds to eat; causing vertigo, blindness, undue fatness, and in many instances death. Here is the recipe from which most of the widely-sold foods are made:

Roasted beef pluck, musty pilot-biscuit, corn meal, ground hemp seed, pulverized sugar made moist with lard.

The ingredients of prepared food for soft-billed birds have always been kept a profound secret by professional bird fanciers; and it cost us $250 to procure the above recipe from a prominent New York manufacturer of bird foods. After we learned it we found, as we had before suspicioned, that it was not only worthless but positively injurious. But it gave us a basis to work on, and after several years' experiment we produced a food the ingredients of which are as follows, only the proper proportions being reserved:

Roasted beef heart, toasted wheat bread, and best quality maw meal; ant eggs, dried sweet potatoes, pea meal, and dried currants; the whole made moist with melted beef suet.

This food is put up in jars holding nearly a pound, and sold by druggists for 35c. The contents of one jar of Prepared Mocking Bird Food will be sent by mail on receipt of 40 cts. Or dry to which the buyer can add the melted suet or lard to make it moist as needed, 25c., by mail 40c.

The principal thing needed to keep soft-billed birds in constant health and song is, first, a good prepared food as a basis, and then variety. The food should be given plain one day; one part, grated carrot (squeezed dry), to three parts, prepared food the next; one part, mashed white potatoes on another; and occasionally one part, grated sweet apple, and three parts prepared food; and so on, varying the diet as much as possible.

Boiled sweet potato is good for them, also boiled milk and ground toasted bread; and a few ant eggs for a change.

Every owner of a soft-billed bird should have a jar of meal worms, and give one or two to his bird every week. Nothing tames a bird so effectually, and in a very short time he will learn to take them from your fingers. They are easily bred by filling an earthen jar about three-quarters full with bits of old leather and bran. Put a hundred or more meal worms in the jar and tie a woolen cloth over the mouth. The cloth must be occasionally wet with water. Meal worms propagate very rapidly, and at the end of three months there will be thousands. These worms will be found under old boards in a pigeon loft or chicken coop, in the meal chest of a barn, or among the lumber of a grist mill. We sell them for 25 cents per hundred.

Shredded lean meat, flies, worms, and spiders are relished by all soft-billed birds, and should be given to them occasionally.

Nearly all birds are fond of bathing, and a dish of water should be placed in the cage at least three times a week; in cold weather it is best to take the chill off the water. When a bird will not go into the bath, dip a wisp-broom in water and flirt it over him.

DISEASES OF CAGE BIRDS.

Almost all the diseases to which cage birds are subject, arise from improper management. If duly fed on the correct foods, their cages regularly cleaned and kept in good air, disease will seldom make its appearance.

Inferior diet, whether seed or prepared food, is the cause of almost all diseases; but colds are another prolific source. How frequently is a bird hung up close to the top corner of a window, with the sash down a foot, and a strong draught of air flowing upon it. Or placed in a room which is warm during the day and cold at night. In these and similar ways many fine birds are killed by taking cold.

Do not give your bird lump sugar or other delicacies. He

will eat them greedily enough, but they will ruin both his health and song.

When a bird is in good health, his feathers are sleek and smooth, adhering close to his body. Whenever you perceive him sitting dull and bunchy, something is out of order.

First, consider if the moulting season is approaching; if anything has frightened him; if he has been hung in a draught; see if he can get at his water and food, and that both are sweet. If none of these is the cause, then compare his symptoms with those printed below, and procure a bottle of **Bird Bitters** from your druggist, and treat him according to the directions wrapped around the bottle. If the patient is a seed-eating bird, get him a **Bird Manna** to use in connection with the liquid.

ASTHMA.—*Symptoms:* Short breath; opening of beak as if to gasp for air, and when frightened keeping it open a long time; and puffing out feathers until the bird has the appearance of a ball.

BLOATING.—The skin on one part, or even the whole body, swells to such a degree that it is stretched like a drum. Pierce with a needle and the air in it will escape.

CATARRH OR COLD.—*Symptoms:* Ruffling of the feathers; nostrils stopped up; tongue hardened by inflammation; beak often open and yellow at base. Use Bird Bitters.

CHRONIC SNEEZING.—*Symptoms:* A constant effort to relieve an accumulation of matter in the nostrils.

CONSTIPATION.—*Symptoms:* Constant and unsuccessful efforts to evacuate, and puffing out of the feathers.

CONSUMPTION.—*Symptoms:* Gradual wasting away, loss of appetite, and cessation of song. If taken in the hand it will appear as light as a feather. Use Bird Manna.

DIARRHŒA.—*Symptoms:* The evacuation frequent and watery, which very soon causes the extreme weakening of the bird. Use Bird Manna and Bird Bitters.

DISLOCATION OF A JOINT may be reduced by gently

stretching the limb and pushing the joint in place, and if done before inflammation sets in the cure is complete.

FITS.—This is a disease that must be treated at once or the bird dies. Pull out one of the smaller tail feathers, cut one of the nails so as to cause it to bleed, and as a last resort plunge the bird into cold water. Use the Bird Bitters according to directions to prevent a recurrence.

INFLAMMATION OF THE BOWELS.—*Symptoms:* Abdomen swollen and covered with red veins; intestines red and swollen; extreme emaciation, ruffling of feathers, and constant sitting with head under the wing.

LONG CLAWS, when they impede the movements of the bird, should be cut. This is a delicate operation; the claw should be held in front of a light so that the veins of the nail can be seen and avoided. Use a sharp pair of scissors.

LOSS OF APPETITE is quickly cured by Bird Bitters or Bird Manna.

LOSS OF SONG, if the bird is otherwise healthy, can be restored by Bird Bitters or Bird Manna.

MOULTING season begins with most birds about the middle of September and lasts for six weeks. During this period birds usually stop singing, as the growth of new feathers makes such a demand upon their system as to render them weak and out of spirits. If a Bird Manna is kept in the cage of a seed-eating bird nine out of ten birds will not stop singing during the entire moulting season. Bird Bitters is most excellent to use as a tonic at this critical period for both soft-billed and seed-eating birds. A few drops put daily in the drinking water will tone them up wonderfully.

PAIRING FEVER usually attacks birds in the spring, about the time the wild birds are mating. They cease to sing and become melancholy. A generous diet should be adopted and the cage placed in a window where the bird can look upon a cheerful scene.

PIP.—*Symptoms:* Roughness of the feathers, drooping of the tail; a tiny white bladder under the feathers, near the vent.

RED MITES.—If your bird looks lean and out of condition, if he is restless—especially at night—and is continually pecking himself, he is infested with mites. Throw a white cloth over his cage at night, and in the morning you will find it covered with tiny red insects. We put up a powder that is perfectly harmless to the birds, but will effectually destroy

the vermin. It is called *Mite Exterminator*, and is sold at 25 cents per package, and can be had of druggists or will be sent by mail. Take the bird gently in your hand, rub the powder over his body, especially under the wings, and at the base of the tail. Before replacing him, put some of the powder in a saucer, drop a coal of fire on it, and place it in the bottom of the cage, covering the latter with a cloth to keep the smoke in, and let it remain for a couple of hours. This will kill all the vermin that are hidden in the cavities of the cage.

SCALES ON THE LEGS can be cured by anointing with Mexican Salve for a week, and then removing carefully with the finger nail

SHEDDING FEATHERS OUT OF SEASON can be stopped by giving Bird Bitters or Bird Manna.

SORE EYES should be washed with the Bird Food Co's Eye Water. Mailed for 25 cents.

SORE FEET arise from dirt or from fine fibres of wool, cotton or silk getting round them and cutting to the bone. Remove the offending substances, clean the perches or bottom of the cage, and wash the feet carefully in lukewarm water, and anoint with Mexican Salve.

SWEATING.—This is a disease peculiar only to hen birds, and attacks them while sitting on their eggs. The belly feathers and the eggs are saturated with perspiration.

SWOLLEN AND SORE LEGS should be bathed with diluted tincture of arnica.

TUMORS should be opened with a sharp knife and the matter pressed out; putting Mexican Salve on the place.

ULCERS are cured by touching them with a red-hot knitting needle, and then anointing with Mexican Salve. Ulcers in the throat should be touched with a feather dipped in a mixture of honey and alum.

UNNATURAL FATNESS is caused in seed-eating birds by too rich food; reduce the quantity given daily, that is put the patient on short allowance until he gets into proper shape again. With soft-billed birds, mix boiled turnips with their food and dry ant-eggs in the drinking water.

VERTIGO OR GIDDINESS.—This is really a habit and not a disease, and is caused by the birds in their endeavors to look up, to turn their head and neck so far around as to cause them to fall off the perch. By simply throwing a dark cloth over the top of the cage a cure is effected.

YELLOW GALL is a small ulcer that forms on the head near the eyes or bill. While the pimple is very minute it can be cured with Bird Bitters or Bird Manna. If it is large when discovered it should be cut off with a sharp knife and the wound anointed with Mexican Salve.

Bird Manna can be had of druggists, or will be sent by mail for 15 cenes. Bird Bitters costs 25 cents per bottle. If it cannot be had of your druggist, it will be sent by mail on receipt of price.

NESTLING FOOD.

Many people are deterred from breeding Canaries and other birds because it is so much trouble to prepare the egg and cracker for the young birds; and this must be made fresh daily, as sour food is sure to be fatal to the young nestlings.

We have by careful experiment succeeded in preparing an egg-food for young birds, which will keep indefinitely and which is actually cheaper than fresh eggs at the average current price. We will guarantee that young birds will thrive on it even better than on the customary cracker and the yolk of hard-boiled eggs. It is ready for immediate use and requires no preparation.

In addition to its use as food for young birds, it is exceedingly beneficial as an adjunct to the ordinary seed diet of all hard-billed birds, and when fed to them once or twice a week will cause a marked improvement in their health and song. Its effect on the health of sick birds is almost magical, and its continued use will often restore the song of birds that have been songless for years.

For soft-billed birds it is an absolute necessity, and a small quantity of it should be given daily in the prepared foods used for this class of songsters.

NESTLING FOOD is worth 25 cents per box; and when sent by mail is 15 cents additional.

THE IN-DOOR AVIARY.

THE Aviary we rarely hear of in an American home, but in Europe there are thousands of by no means wealthy people whose delight it is to keep, to rear, and to study birds. There, a gentleman's mansion is no more complete without an Aviary than it would be here without a conservatory.

But the custom of keeping birds is growing in this country in a surprising manner, and it will not be many years before the pleasing practice will be as popular on this side as it is on the other side of the Atlantic.

The room selected for the Aviary should have a sunny aspect and be well protected from draughts. Arrangements should be made to have it heated in winter either by steam register, or a gas or oil stove will answer, surrounded by wire netting, so that the birds cannot fly against it and burn themselves. If a conservatory or similar glass structure is to be used, it should be well shaded from strong sunlight avoiding as far as possible all extremes in temperature.

Having selected a suitable room, furnish it with a number of small Christmas trees, selecting such as have flat, spreading branches; and arrange them tastefully, singly or in clumps, filling up corners, etc. If these trees are taken up in the spring or autumn and planted in wooden tubs, they will grow and keep green for nearly a year, and can then be replaced by fresh ones.

FIG. 2.—CIGAR-BOX NEST BOX.

In addition to the trees, a few fantastically-arranged dead branches of trees; old gnarled stumps and roots can be placed where they will be the most effective. If it is desired to keep and breed parrots or parroquets, procure the trunks of trees, in which bore, at different heights, several augur holes, both large and small ones.

FIG. 3.—HOLLOW TREE NEST BOX.

Regarding nesting places, the majority of the birds will select the trees, but it is well to have a few boxes of different patterns scattered about to accomodate such birds as prefer them.

A wire nest, arranged for fastening against the wall, will be sent by mail for 12c. each. Fig. No. 2 is an excellent pattern which you can make yourself from a cigar box. Fig. No. 3 is made from a portion of a small tree trunk, hollowed-out and with a hole bored in the side. This style is for parrots, parroquets, and other climbing birds. Fig. No. 4 is made from the husk of a cocoanut, and is suitable for African Finches and other species of tropical birds.

Furnish a good supply of nesting materials, such as, fibrous roots, long, fine, dry grass, Florida moss, soft cow's hair, and soft feathers. The hair, moss, and feathers should be suspended in nets; if allowed to lie about they will become soiled and unfit for nest-building. Cotton and wool should not be used, as both are liable to become entangled in the feet of the birds, and cause them

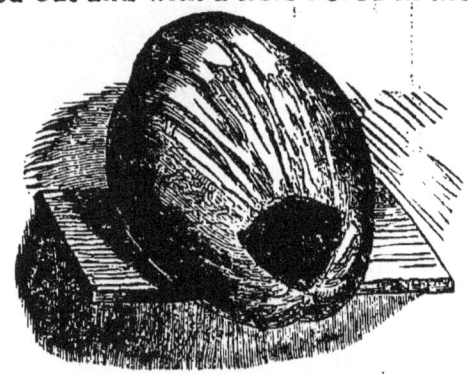

FIG. 4.—COCOANUT-HUSK NEST BOX.

to lose their toes and sometimes their legs by this means.

The floor should be strewn with coarse white sand, which should be renewed frequently. Plenty of cuttle-bone should always be kept within easy reach of the birds.

The seeds with which the birds are fed should not be strewn over the floor, but kept in a self-feeding hopper, as shown in Figs. Nos. 5 and 6. This can be made by any carpenter, or we can supply them in different sizes, from $2.00 to $10.00 each. This hopper is hung against the wall, so as to be inaccessible to mice. Fresh sods placed daily in the Aviary will furnish much amusement to the birds, and

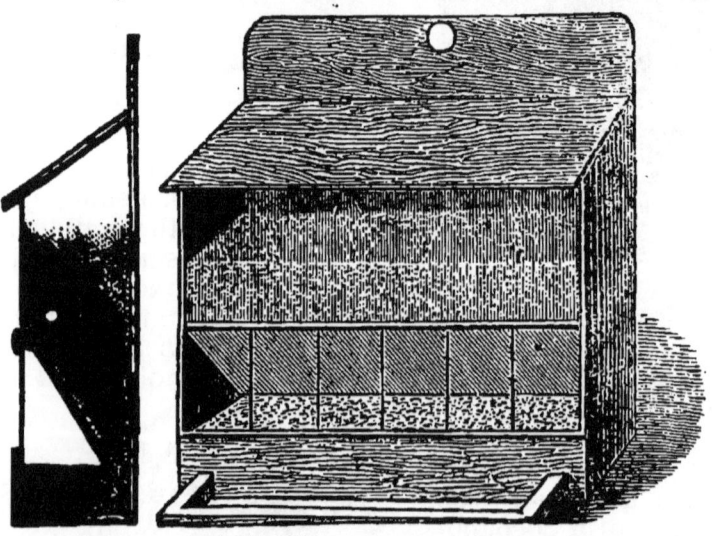

FIG. 5.—SELF-FEEDING HOPPER.—FIG. 6.
SIDE VIEW.   FRONT VIEW.

be, besides, highly beneficial to their health. The food of soft-billed birds should be kept in a shallow tin tray, with a cover over the top to keep the birds from soiling the contents. The sides of the tray should be open, to provide access to the food.

Whenever practicable, a fountain with running water should be introduced; but where this is impossible, drinking fountains of the pattern shown in Fig. No. 7 should be used. These are made of stone, and we can supply them at the following prices: one quart, 35c.; half-gallon, 70c.; gallon, $1.00; two gallons, $1.50.

Bathing is, of course, very essential; and no vessel is more suitable for the purpose than a large shallow dish; and this should be introduced for an hour or two every day.

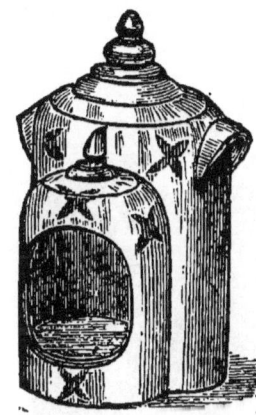

FIG. 7.—DRINKING FOUNTAIN.

In such a room as described, soft-billed and seed-eating birds will live amicably together, make sweet music, and build nests and rear their young. Should any bird or pair of birds prove on introduction into an Aviary to be quarrelsome with their associates, remove it or them at once before some of the smaller birds are killed or nests and eggs destroyed. A mischievous bird will sometimes do untold damage in an Aviary.

By carefully reading the articles on the different kinds of birds, you can form a very fair idea of what varieties are suitable for the Aviary. We are always willing to aid in the selection of the various birds when desired.

The Fronefield's Cattle Powder Co., 346 Dillwyn St., Philadelphia, Pa., will send by mail, FREE, a valuable package of their famous Cattle Powder to every farmer who applies. The original, the oldest, the strongest and the best made. It may save you hundreds of dollars.

THE OUT-DOOR AVIARY.

An Aviary built on a lawn and made in a style somewhat similar to that shown in the engraving, is one of the most interesting additions to a country-place that can be devised.

There are many species of foreign and domestic birds that will readily stand the cold of the most rigorous winter. In such an Aviary we have seen Canaries flying about and gayly singing amid a January snow-storm. In the out-door Aviary matting should be hung on the sides exposed to the north and east winds, and perches should be erected under the conical roof, to which the birds can retreat when the cold is the greatest. Care should be taken in frosty weather to see that the ice is broken in the drinking fountain, so that the birds do not suffer from thirst. If preferred, glass sashes can be fitted on the outside of the wires, and then the birds will not be exposed to the severe storms that prevail in some latitudes during the winter. Birds reared in an out-

OUT-DOOR AVIARY.

door Aviary will be much healthier and the percentage of deaths less than when reared in-doors.

AVIARY CAGES.

No. 1.

In homes where the necessary room cannot be spared for a properly-arranged Aviary, one of the large cages herewith illustrated will answer for a substitute that will be a constant source of interest and amusement. In these cages a number of different kinds of birds can be kept, and will live in harmony. If the proper foods are supplied, both hard and soft billed birds can be kept together in one cage.

Cage No. 1 is made of brass wires, set closely together so as to retain the smallest African Finch; with base of oiled black walnut. It is 30 inches high, 35 inches long, and 14½ inches wide. It will comfortably accommodate about 35 birds. Price, $27.00.

Cage No. 2, is made of close brass wires and black walnut box. It is made of two sizes, as follows: 14½ by 23½ in. It will accommodate about 30 birds. Price, with dome, $21.00; without dome, $18.00. Size, 20x29 inches. It will accommodate about 40 birds. Price, with dome, $40.00; without dome, $35.00.

Cage No. 3 is made of close brass wires with black walnut base.

No. 2.

Size, 14½ x 17¼ in. It will accommodate about 20 birds. Price, $7.00.

We will also make to order Aviary Cages of any size, with walnut frame and tinned iron wires, at reasonable prices. These cages can be made of any shape to fit-in between windows or in corners.

No. 3.

TRAPPING BIRDS.

The trapping of song and game birds is forbidden by special law in most of the states. The laws of the state of New York do not however protect the English sparrow, the crow, the hawk, the crane, the raven, the crow black bird, the common blackbird nor the kingfisher. These may be trapped in many ways. One of the best is by the use of the trap-cage here with illustrated. A bird of the same species that it is desired to capture is placed in the lower part of the cage. The trap is then set, and some attractive food scattered about.

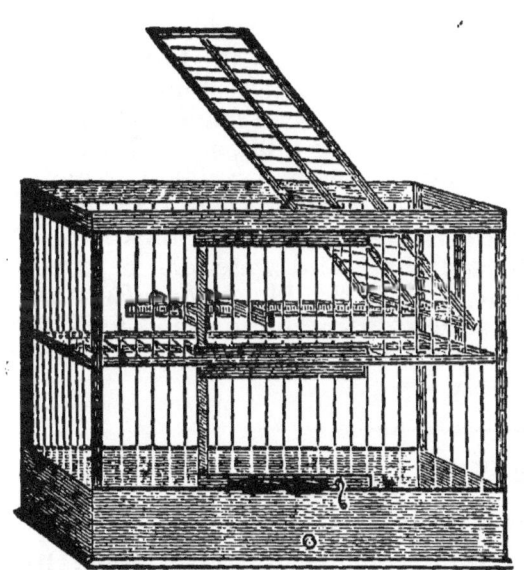

Bird Lime is the easiest and surest way of trapping. We supply it, already prepared, for 25 cents per can, 10 cents extra by mail. The manner of using it is very simple. A bundle of long elastic switches are cut from a willow or birch tree, smeared over with the Bird Lime, and stuck into the ground, a few inches apart, in the form of an oval. Inside of this a live bird is placed, with its wings fastened to its body by means of a rubber band, or a stuffed bird can be used. The bushes and lower branches of near growing trees, upon which the birds are likely to alight, should also be coated with the Bird Lime. Tempting food should be scattered about the limed switches. As soon as the feet, wings, or feathers of a bird touch the Bird Lime, he is held a prisoner, and should be taken-off at once, before his plumage becomes coated with the sticky substance. A stuff'd owl will attract hosts of small birds to the limed twigs. We can furnish stuffed specimens of almost any variety of small birds, and send them by mail for $1.25 each; owls, $3.50 each.

When birds are first put into a cage, a rubber band should be slipped over their body and wings, to prevent them fluttering, and the cages placed in a darkened room, away from all bustle and noise, until they become accustomed to cage life.

Soft-billed birds make better songsters and become more tame, when taken from the nest, just as the tail feathers begin to grow, and raised by hand. They should be kept in a soft cotton nest, and fed upon a paste made as follows: Upon stale wheat bread pour boiling milk, and after it becomes soft, squeeze dry, and mix with the yolk of a hard-boiled egg, and a little finely-shredded lean raw meat. This must be prepared fresh every day. Nestlings should be fed a little at a time, but often, and water can be dropped into their open mouths from a quill. Even after they can feed themselves, it is advisable to continue hand-feeding; as it makes them grow more rapidly, and keeps them in good condition.

STUFFING BIRDS.

People who have become attached to a bird, generally desire to have it stuffed when it dies; but those who live remote from cities, have hitherto been unable to have this done. We are able to obviate this difficulty by giving directions for preserving the dead body, so that it can be sent from anywhere in the United States, reached by express, and it will come to us sufficiently preserved to stuff. As soon as the bird dies, inject into its throat and anus, by means of a syringe, a weak solution of carbolic acid, care being taken not to get any on the plumage. Then pack it in crushed charcoal, and send to us by express. The charge for stuffing a bird, the size of a Canary, is $1.00; one as large as a Robin, $1.50, the size of an Owl $3.50. The price of stuffing animals varies from $1.00 to $100. Glass shades for mounted Canaries, to keep off the dust, are worth $1.00 each; next size, $1.50, and a size large enough for an Owl, $3.00.

We can supply almost all species of birds and animals for

collections, mounted in the most artistic and life-like manner at prices ranging from 50c to $100.

Money must accompany all birds or animals sent to us to be stuffed.

PROPER CARE OF CANARIES.

The best food for Canaries is our Mixed Seed, and plenty of red gravel strewn on the bottom of the cage and renewed daily. A cuttle-bone should always be kept in the cage, and also a Bird Manna. A bit of chickweed, a slice of apple, and a ripe fig may be given occasionally; but only as a treat, and not oftener than once a week.

Never give them sugar, apple, cake, or other dainties. It makes them too fat, spoils their voice and causes them to go out of song. A bath should be given every day, if they will take one; in cold weather the chill should be taken off the water. Hang the cage where no draft will strike it. Canaries can stand almost any degree of cold, but a draft is fatal. When they are moulting (shedding feathers), if it is desired to have them continue singing, feed them twice a week on our *Nestling Food* in addition to their seed diet, and keep a *Bird Manna* constantly in their cage. They cease singing at this season, from weakness caused by the growth of new feathers, and the foods mentioned above strengthen them so much that they will continue in song even after they have lost nearly all their plumage. The moulting season begins in September and continues about six weeks. Birds that moult out of season do so from weakness or from having caught cold by being kept in an uneven temperature or the cage is placed in a draft.

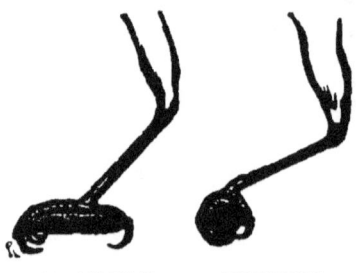

COMFORT.   MISERY.

The engravings numbered 1 and 2 will furnish an ocular demonstration of how easy it is to inflict constant punishment on a bird bone by having a cage which is fitted up with unsuitable perches.

BREEDING CANARIES.

Canaries may be mated during the months of January, February, March, April, and May. The breeding cage shown in the engraving is a most excellent style. It is made of walnut, with tinned wires; and the price with nests, hair, and everything ready for breeding, is $1.25. The long breeds of Canaries require a somewhat higher cage, which is worth $2.75. In mating a pair of Canaries all that is necessary is to put the male and female together in a breeding cage and hang it in some quiet corner, about five feet from the floor. At first the male may fight with the female, or *vice versa*, but this quarreling is usually of short durat:on, and they will soon settle quietly down to the routine of bird housekeeping.

There should always be placed in the mating-cage a piece of cuttle-bone for the formation of shell, or the hen may lay soft-shell eggs. There is also required deer's or cow's hair for the construction of the nest. To the seed diet of the mated birds, should be added hard-boiled egg and cracker, rolled fine; or our Nestling Food, a little each day.

If the birds have access to Bird Manna, they will feed it to their nestlings, and a more rapid growth will result, and a wonderful decrease in the number of deaths will be noticed

When the male begins to feed the female, you may rest assured that all is going as it should, and now is the time to put a little cow's hair between the wires of the cage. Do not put in much at a time, however, as the birds will scatter it over the bottom of the cage and render it unfit for use.

If for some unknown reason the birds take a dislike to each other and will not mate, it will be necessary to try and discover which one is in fault, and substitute another bird.

Two hens can be mated to one male by using a cage with a movable wire partition, fitted up with two sets of nests. Such a cage is worth $2.50. In this kind of breeding cage put the male with one female in one side of the cage, and after the hen has laid all her eggs, put the second hen in the other

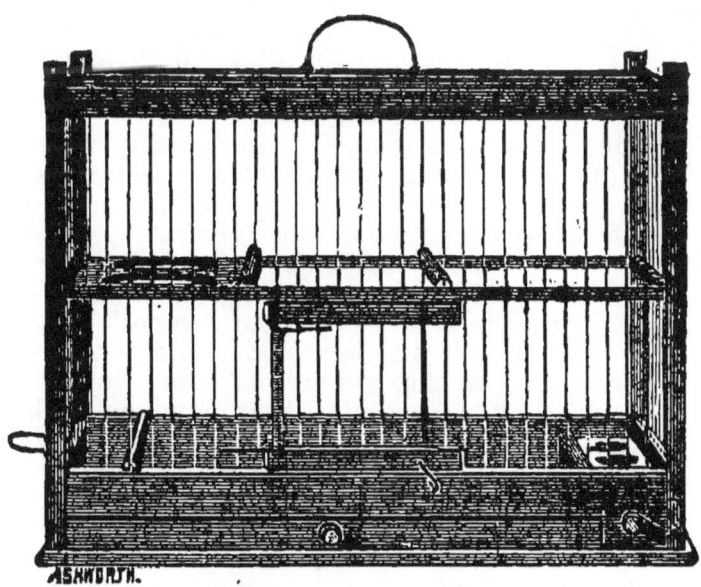

BREEDING CAGE.

side with the male; after she also has laid her eggs the partition can be taken out and the male will help to hatch and feed both nests.

After having been mated about a week, the hen will begin to lay one egg each day, until from four to six eggs are laid; upon these she will sit from fourteen to sixteen days, when the eggs should hatch, and in the order in whch they were laid. Never disturb the eggs, or they may not hatch. During the period of incubation, the male relieves the female by sitting on the nest, a few hours each day. Should either of them become addicted to the vice of breaking the eggs, they should be bountifully fed with egg and bread, which should be constantly kept within their reach. Should they still persist, the eggs can be removed as fast as laid. and their places supplied with eggs whittled from chalk. When the hen ceases to lay, then return the eggs and all will go well.

Three days before the hatching of the first egg, feed the bird in addition to her seed, half a hard-boiled egg grated, and mixed with cracker dust or prepared "*Nestling Food*," and continue this diet until the nestlings are old enough to take care of themseves. Instead of putting this soft food in a saucer, as is the usual costom, have a tinner make a little tin box, as shown in the engraving.

The young birds when weaned from the old birds should be placed in a cage entirely away, otherwise fretfulness is encouraged, which it is well to avoid. A wire partition will do for a day or so when they are first separated, so that the old birds can feed them through the wires. When caging-off young birds give them at first grated egg and cracker, or our *Nestling Food*. When they are about a month old, introduce seed in the cage in a separate pot or tin, with the view of giving the birds an opportunity of finding out what the seed is intended for. Generally, when about six weeks old, the young Canaries begin to shell the seed, and at that time the proportion of soft food may be gradually diminished until the seed at length takes the place of the egg and cracker An increase of seed shells upon the cage bottom will be a guide in reducing the quantity of soft food.

When the young birds are two or three weeks old, and can eat alone, and sometimes before quitting the nest, the males commence swelling out their throats and trying to warble. The sexes may thus be distinguished, as the females seldom try to warble, and when they do, it is always in a less marked degree than the males.

If it is desired to make very fine singers of the young males, as fine as the highly vaunted Andreasberg Rollers, they should be put in small wire cages, separated from each other, covered entirely over with coverings of muslin, so that they can see no external objects and yet have sufficient light to feed by. These cages should be arranged around the walls of a room, the only tenants of which are fine singing birds, such as nightingales, linnets, skylarks, black caps, etc., and one or two Andreasberg Rollers, or other trained Canaries. The young birds will acquire the fine notes of some or all of the other birds. Of course the longer they are kept at such a school the more proficient they will become.

If a young Canary is hung in a darkened cage, out of hearing of the song of all other birds, and some simple air played to him on a flute, piano, or organ, three or four times a day, he will readily pick up all or a portion of it, and add it to his repertoire of notes.

There are various points to be observed, and to contend with while breeding Canaries. By meddling too much with the nests or eggs, or allowing strangers to pry about your birds during nesting, restless hens will often forsake their nests and young. The young are sometimes killed in the egg by loud or near noises; such as thunder, the firing of a gun, slamming of a door, etc.

A vitiated atmosphere will encourage uneasiness in hens, and sometimes cause them to leave their nests.

Some hens and males will occasionally pick and maim the nestlings. This is usually caused by vermin that prey upon the parents and irritate them, making them peevish and fretful.

After the young birds are fourteen days old it is always best to put them in a clean nest and destroy the old one which by this time usually infested by vermin.

When eggs are infertile it is nine times out of ten the fault of the male, and another should be substituted.

Hens, especially young ones, just prior to laying appear dull, and sometimes so weak as to be unable to reach the nest. When this is the case apply a little sweet oil on a feather to the vent, and place the hen on her nest. Holding her over the steam of a kettle for a few seconds also aids in the ejection of the egg.

When the breeding cage is hung in a very warm and dry room it will be beneficial on the day before the young birds are due to take each one out of the nest with a spoon and dip it into tepid water.

To produce handsome, yellow birds, the male should be a pale yellow, and the female a deep yellow bird. A clear yellow bird, mated with a very deep green hen, will probably have handsome mottled young. A very deep yellow male, mated with a very deep green or brown hen, often produce the highly prized Cinnamon bird.

Never allow two crested birds to pair, as their progeny are likely to be bald or malformed about the head.

BREEDING CANARIES IN A ROOM, UN-CAGED.

Canaries will breed famously if turned loose in a room; and where no single variety is kept and no particular excellence aimed at, there is no better plan, or one more adapted to furnish the largest amount of pleasure at the least expense. The birds have more scope for freedom of action in a room than in a cage.

No artificial heat is needed as Canaries will stand almost any amount of cold, providing there is no draught.

Do not mate them before turning them loose, but it is better to have at least twice as many females as males. Each male will pair with some particular hen and pay her special attention, at least till she is sitting, when the chances are he will court some new flame; but he will not neglect his first love, and will continue to feed her on the nest, though, under the circumstances, he will become general in his attentions. And it is strange to note the behavior of hens in an aviary. Two will sometimes sit on the edge of a nest feeding as assiduously as if each claimed the young ones for her own.

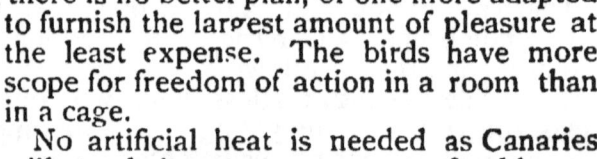

FIG. 1.

By all means introduce male linnets; and goldfinches, either males or hens. Hen linnets will breed in rooms only under special treatment, and then very rarely; but a hen goldfinch will build, sit, hatch, and feed as well as a canary. The progeny will be linnet and canary mules, and goldfinch and canary mules; and will in all probability be dark solid-colored birds. The hens will be useless, but the males are excellent songsters.

Range some Christmas trees around the walls and in the middle of the room. If, in addition to these, you can get any old roots or any such rough material, to place against or hang on the wall, you will find the birds will soon select the snug corners and begin to build. Give a supply of moss, soft hay, any bunch of fibrous roots you may meet with, or similar material, with which they will build the foundation of their nests; and plenty of soft doe hair. Add some rabbit-down, with which they will put the finishing touch to a nest.

We illustrate two styles of nest boxes; No. 1 any tinner will make for you, and No. 2 you can make yourself out of cigar-box lids. We will send by mail, nest baskets of wire, ready for nailing against the wall, for 12 cents each.

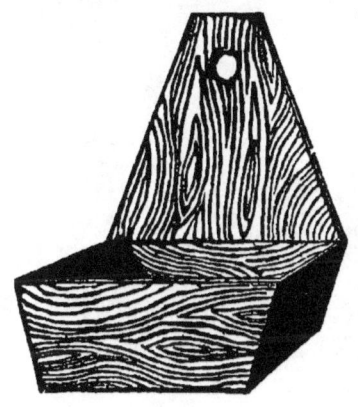

FIG. 2.

BREEDING CANARIES FOR PROFIT.

Besides being a most fascinating pastime Canary breeding when conducted intelligently, systematically, and on a sufficiently-large scale can be made a source of considerable profit. The spare time that nearly every man has before and after business is amply sufficient to care for even a hundred pairs of Canaries; and the business is one that is especially suitable to be engaged in by women.

Canaries are always in demand, and the better class of singers, the different fancy varieties, and especially mule birds are scarce and consequently command ready sale and high prices. Like breeding every other kind of live stock, the best is always the most remunerative, and we advise all who intend embarking in Canary breeding as a business, if they intend rearing singers, to select only the best singing males they can procure, mate them with females from St. Andreasberg, Germany, and to have a collection of wild singing birds, and the best grade of Andreasberg Rollers as teachers. When the young birds cannot be disposed of to

ROOM ARRANGED FOR BREEDING CANARIES.

advantage in the breeder's own vicinity, the bird dealers of the large cities will always pay fair prices for good stock. It always pays best to hold the singers until May before selling, as by that time the importation of German birds ceases for the season, and Canaries are then very scarce, and command the highest prices of the year. The females should be sold about January, when they are in demand, and prices reach the highest point. The cost of feeding is only a trifle for each bird, and the percentage of deaths when the birds are properly cared for is very small; so that the stock can be carried to the season mentioned above with but little expense and risk.

The fancy varieties and mule birds it is best to sell as soon as they are matured. The prices for these remain about the same the year around; but the demand is always greater in the Spring than at other seasons of the year.

Cayenne-fed Canaries are becoming fashionable, and as this artificial coloring can be done by the breeder without risk, it will be remunerative to thus color some of the young birds at their second moult, and reap the advantage of the high price such specimens are worth.

In breeding Canaries on a large scale it is a great advantage to devote a room to the purpose, arranging the cages around the sides of the wall, as is shown in the full page engraving opposite.

MULE BIRDS.

The mating of Canaries with the different species of cage birds and the rearing of mules is a most interesting pastime. There is the same sort of fascination about it that there is in investing in a lottery ticket. There is a chance of drawing a valuable prize, but candor causes us to admit that in mule breeding as in a lottery there are more blanks drawn than prizes.

A female Canary will mate with many species of wild birds, and the young males resulting from the cross will be superb singers, or of fine plumage; in many instances both. The female mules are useless and will seldom breed. In mule breeding we advise that the birds be not mated earlier than May, and that the same general advice be followed as we have previously given regarding the breeding of

Canaries. We now give a list of the names of birds that will mate with the Canary.

LINNET AND CANARY—Use only a male Linnet. The mules resemble in plumage an ordinary green or gray Canary but the males are superb songsters and very imitative, quickly learning the notes of any bird that is within hearing and adding thereto their own song. This is also so, but in a less degree with nearly all mule birds. A Linnet mule in song is worth from $5 to $50.

GOLDFINCH AND CANARY.—Either a male or female Goldfinch can be used, the former being preferable. The males are of most striking plumage, and are fine songsters. This is the easiest and most successful of all crosses. A male Goldfinch mule in song is worth from $5 to $75.

GOLDFINCH AND LINNET.—A male Linnet will sometimes mate with a female Goldfinch, and the result is a rare mule bird of curious plumage and fine song. These mules are so rare that no prices can be quoted for them.

GOLDFINCH AND BULLFINCH.—This cross requires a male Bullfinch and female Goldfinch, and is even rarer than the one just mentioned. No price can be quoted.

BULLFINCH AND CANARY.—A female Canary will sometimes mate with a male Bullfinch. The mule birds are of beautiful plumage, have an indifferent natural song, but can be taught airs much easier than the Bullfinch proper.

GREENFINCH AND CANARY.—This is not a difficult cross to make, but the resulting mule birds are not very valuable.

SISKIN AND CANARY.—Use a male Siskin and a female Canary. This is a very easy cross to make, and the mule birds are quite pleasing songsters.

CHAFFINCH AND CANARY.—From the fact that the Chaffinch is larger and stronger than the Canary, he is apt in mating to frighten the latter badly, and cause her to abandon her idea of nesting. The cross is sometimes successfully accomplished, but the result hardly warrants the trouble, the mules being of but little account.

Many of our hard billed native birds can be successfully crossed with Canaries. There are many well authenticated instances where mule birds have been raised from a cross with the American Goldfinch or Thistle bird, the Nonpareil, the Indigo bird, the Bobolink, the Banana bird, and many others.

DIFFERENT VARIETIES OF CANARIES.

More than three hundred years ago a ship sailing from the Canary Islands, laden with merchandise, and having on board a few Canaries, was wrecked on the coast of Italy. The birds escaped to the timbered lands near the shore, where they bred freely, and would have become naturalized had not the sweetness of their song attracted the natives, who were possessed of so strong a desire to obtain them that all were soon captured. The progeny of these birds spread rapidly over all Europe.

THE GERMAN, OR SONG CANARY.

The song Canary is now bred principally in Germany, among the Hartz Mountains of Hanover, where the peasants' chief means of subsistence is the breeding of these feathered musicians for the markets of the world

The peasants manufacture small wooden cages from the fir wood which grows upon the mountain sides, and every bird has a separate cage made entirely of wood; pegs instead of nails are used to fasten them together. In these little cages the birds are shipped to this country, and are kept in their narrow quarters until bought to make American homes cheerful with their merry music. It is estimated that about one hundred thousand Canaries are imported annually into America. During the passage across the ocean they require careful attention in feeding and watering. The cages are arranged in divisions, so as to allow the attendant to pass between them to feed the birds and clean the cages. If cleanliness is neglected sickness is engendered, and many birds perish in consequence.

TOPKNOT CANARY.

The male canary is the songster. The female scarcely ever sings, and when she does her notes are weak. The male has a short, stout beak and a flat head, and is wide between the eyes, the wider the better. The crown of the head of the female is more round than that of the male.

A fallacy quite prevalent in some parts of the country is, that dark-colored canaries are the strongest birds and the best singers. Color in canaries has no more to do with their singing qualities than complexion has with the voice of the prima donna.

In selecting a Canary it should be borne in mind that the feet and legs of young birds are smooth and glossy, and the toe-nails are short; whereas, old birds have rough and scaly feet, with long toe-nails.

In Europe great attention is paid to improving the song of Canaries. To attain this result two modes are practiced. A large cage is constructed with close partitions which ef-

DIFFERENT TYPES OF CRESTS.

fectually exclude the view from each other; a superior singing Canary, a nightingale, or skylark, is placed within nearing, but out of sight of the Canaries, who learn to imitate the melodious notes they hear. In six months they will have acquired perfection, when they are removed to separate cages. The other method is, when the young birds first try to sing they are separated from the parent bird, and placed in a room where just light enough is admitted to enable them to see to eat. Then a musical instrument called a bird organ, is played for an hour each day in the hearing of the young bird. If undisturbed, they become attentive listeners, and by practicing the song, are soon able to reproduce it perfectly.

These trained birds are known as Andreasberg Rollers, and the finest of them have no "chop" notes, and are proficient in what are known as the water roll, the bell, and the flute notes.

Both the Andreasberg Roller and the Hartz Mountain canary can be procured of several colors: deep yellow, light yellow, green, and mottled; and they are both plain-headed, and with a crest of feathers on the head

IMPORTED GERMAN CANARIES vary in price according to the season. From October until April *males in full song* are worth $2.50; and the remainder of the season, $3.00.

THE WONDERFUL NIGHT-SINGING CANARIES, which sing as well by lamp-light as during the day, are worth $3 each.

ANDREASBERG ROLLERS come in three grades; the lowest, which are much superior to the ordinary German Canary, and are worth $4.00 each; the next grade is worth $5.00; and the highest grade, which are the best singers in the world, are $8.00 each.

IMPORTED FEMALE CANARIES are worth $1.00.

THE RED, OR CAYENNE, CANARIES.

These birds are the ordinary German Canary, whose plumage has been artificially colored by systematically feeding, prior to and during the time of shedding feathers, on crackers and eggs, highly seasoned with cayenne pepper. This color, which is a most beautiful red tint, is retained until the bird moults, when the cayenne feeding must be renewed or the plumage will come in of the ordinary yellow. No harm is done by this hot diet to either health or song. Any Canary can be thus artificially colored, but care must be taken in the selection of the pepper, as all commercial red pepper is adulterated with substances that are very likely to kill the bird. We have pepper specially ground for this purpose. Full directions accompany each can, which contains sufficient to last the bird during the time of moulting. Price, 25c. per can; if sent by mail, add 12c. for postage.

CAYENNE COLORED CANARIES, in full song, are worth from $6.00 to $18.00 each, according to the perfection of the plumage

THE AMERICAN-BRED CANARY.

The Canaries which are bred in this country are, as a rule, neither so fine or constant singers as their German cousins. The reason of this is from the fact that those who breed Canaries here, are not careful in the selection of stock. To secure fine songsters it is necessary to have an excellent singing male bird mated to a female from a strain that is known to be singers; and then to have a superior songster to teach the young birds.

It is so seldom that we can get good American-bred singers, that it is useless to quote prices.

American-bred females are worth 50c.; and from superior stock, 75c. each.

THE CINNAMON CANARY.

The name of this variety is indicative of its color, which principally distinguishes it from the German variety. It has also pink eyes, which are found in no other breed of Canaries. They are most excellent songsters, and are often taught to execute the flute and water roll as well as the Andreasberg Roller. Some specimens have fine, large crest, and very prettily marked mottles are often met with, which are the result of a cross with the ordinary yellow Canary.

Solid Cinnamon Canaries males, in song, are worth $4.00 to $10.00; females, $2.00 to $5.00. Cinnamon mottles males, in song, are worth $3.00 to $8.00 females, $1.00 to $4.00.

A Cinnamon Male Canary mated with a deep yellow hen will produce beautiful mottled and very rich, solid cinnamon young ones.

THE NORWICH CANARY.

This variety is very compact in form and plumage, and is much prized for its beautiful color. They are very robust, free in song, and generally possessed of a bold voice. If well tutored none but the German Canary can surpass them for melody. They are bred of several different colors, the most admired of which is deep orange-yellow; besides which are buff, mealy, deep green and variegated colors. The crested variety which comes in all the above mentioned colors, has a larger, fuller crest than any other breed of Canaries, that in a perfect specimen falls over the eyes, so as to nearly obscure the sight.

The Norwich is the hardiest of all Canaries, and will stand a greater degree of cold than any other.

Male Norwich Canaries are worth from $4 to $12 each; females, $2 to $10.

THE FRENCH CANARY.

This breed of Canaries somewhat resembles the Belgian, but is smaller and more slender. The feathers of the breast are ruffled, giving a most odd appearance to the bird. They are bred of all the Canary colors; and with crest, and plain-headed.

The illustration shows a French Canary with an eye mark, which by professional fanciers is considered a point of great beauty.

They are generally better singers than the Belgian, but are still not to be recommended for their musical qualities.

The French, as well as all long breeds of Canaries, should be kept in taller and roomier cages than ordinary Canaries, so that their peculiar shape will be shown to advantage.

French Canaries, males, are worth $3.00 to $15.00; females, $2.00 to $12.00.

THE SCOTCH FANCY CANARY.

This Canary is in every way a most remarkable variety, and as its name suggests, was created in Scotland. In size it resembles the Belgian, but the outline of the shape of a good specimen closely approximates a perfect half circle. They are bred of all colors, but the deep yellow is the most attractive. Their song is about on a par with that of the French variety.

Scotch Canaries, males, are worth, $12.00 to $20.00; females, $10.00 to $18.00.

THE BELGIAN CANARY.

The Belgian Canary is without doubt the most delicate, and at the same time, the most highly prized of any variety. They are truly noble birds, and any one who has ever possessed a pure-bred bird—not one of the so-called Belgian, which are so often seen, shapeless creatures without one of the characteristics of the true breed, but a bird with "thoroughbred" stamped all over him—will at once admit that having acquired a taste for the variety, all others are thought very little of. They will stand and look at you without flinching, and draw near to you when you approach their cage; they seem to endeavor to show their gratitude for your kind care and attention. This is the case with young birds; even from the nest they do not seem shy, and never fly wildly about the cage every time the person in the habit of feeding them comes near. They certainly require more care and attention than the common Canaries, but they amply repay this, as a really good specimen will attract universal attention, and is something to be proud of.

BELGIAN CANARY.

They are bred of all colors common to the Canary family, but clear yellow is the one generally esteemed the most.

Belgian Canaries, males, are worth $5.00 to $25.00; females, $4.00 to $20.00.

Their voice is rather weak and wavering, and their song is short.

THE YORKSHIRE CANARY.

This is also an English breed of the long Canary, and resembles the French variety in shape and size, but lacks the ruffles on the breast that is characteristic of the latter. They are both plain-headed and crested and are bred of all the ordinary colors.

Yorkshire Canaries, males, are worth, $12.00 to $20.00; females, $10.00 to $18.00.

THE LONDON FANCY CANARY.

In all characteristics except the markings of the plumage, the London Fancy Canary closely resembles the ordinary breed. The body color of the best specimens is a deep orange, with which the black or dark flight feathers and tail contrast most beautifully. The young birds before the first moult resemble an ordinary green Canary, and it is only after they shed their next feathers that the characteristics of the breed show. After a year or so the black feathers are replaced by yellow ones, until finally the bird becomes to all appearances an ordinary yellow or mottled bird. The beak, claws, and legs of this variety should be dark.

The quality of their song is only ordinary, and they are kept and bred only for their beauty and novelty.

London Fancy Canaries, males, are worth $6.00 to $15.00; females, $5.00 to $10.00.

THE LIZARD CANARY.

The Lizard Canary, so named from a fancied resemblance of its green plumage, spotted with yellow, to the color of a lizard, is held in high estimation by Canary fanciers generally. They are stout, short, rather thick-set birds. In plumage, the top of the head in a line from the top of the beak, across the eyes and evenly around the back of the head, must be clear yellow; this is called the cap. The rest of plumage is green or gray, with spots of yellow on the tips of the feathers of the back, wing, and upper tail coverts. Lizard canaries are divided by fanciers into three classes: Golden Spangled, Silver Spangled, and Blue Spangled, the latter of which is the rarest. The Golden Spangled has much green in the ground color, the cap and spangles being of a deep yellow. In the Silver Spangled the ground color nearly approaches a gray, with the cap and spangles of a very pale yellow. When the

HEAD OF LIZARD CANARY.

ground color presents a bluish-gray cast such specimens are called Blue Lizards.

In breeding Lizard Canaries the best results are produced by mating a Gold Spangled and Silver Spangled together. Until the young birds shed their nest feathers they look exactly like a common gray or green canary, with a yellow cap; the spangles being absent.

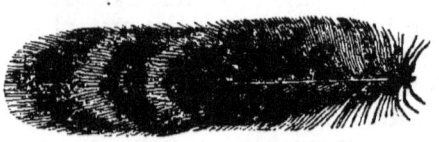

FEATHER FROM BACK.

As they advance in age they grow lighter in color, so that they are in the final plumage when a year old. As songsters they are only ordinary.

Lizard Canaries, males, are worth $5.00 to $12.00; females $4.00 to $10.00.

THE MANCHESTER COPPY.

The Manchester, or, as it is sometimes called, Lancashire Coppy Canary, is the largest of all breeds. There is considerable grace in a good specimen, bearing a large crest on its head, and standing fearless and stately. The longer the birds are, and the better the crests, the more they are prized. Their song, although loud, is not very musical.

In breeding "Coppies" the same rule applies as with all other crested varieties. Mate a plain-headed bird with a crested one to produce the best results.

LANCASHIRE COPPY.

Males Manchester Coppies are worth $10.00 to $25.00; females, $8.00 to $20.00.

THE GOLDFINCH.

In Europe this bird ranks next to the Canary as a popular cage bird, but in this country he has not, as yet, received the attention he deserves.

The Goldfinch is possessed of an exceedingly sweet song, combining a clear metallic ring with modulated power, much softer and sweeter than the Canary's, and linked together by a continued twittering, making the song last for a long time without intermission.

In the male bird the front of the head is blood-red; and the same color, with an intervening ring of black surrounds the base of the beak. The cheeks and front of the throat are white, while the whole back is a ruddy brown. The pinion feathers are jet black, tipped with white. There is also a golden stripe along each pinion. The tail is black and forked. The female is not as large as the male, and not so vividly red about the beak; nor is the black line that divides the red poll from the red beak so intense. The white of her cheeks is intermixed with brown. Altogether, she is not bright and sparkling, and has not such bold, bright eyes as her mate.

The Goldfinch is one of the most docile and intelligent of birds. When properly instructed, it will draw up its food and water. It is taught this by means of a chain and pulley, furnished with a soft, leather band, pierced with four holes, through which the wings and feet are passed; the two ends meeting under the belly, and sustained there by a ring, to which is fastened the chain, that supports a little tin bucket containing the seed or water. Whenever the Goldfinch wants either, he draws up the chain with his beak, fixing it at intervals with his foot, and thus obtains what he wishes;

but if two buckets are suspended to a pully, raising one makes the other descend, and it can only obtain seed and water in turn.

The Goldfinch is of a restless disposition, continually hopping about and clinging to the wires of the cage, and rattling against them.

When in the aviary it sometimes acts in a domineering manner, driving the other birds from the seed; but will seldom fight, although often showing ill-temper.

There are several varieties of Goldfinches that differ in some slight respects from each other. The one known as the White-legged Goldfinch is larger than the ordinary variety, and has white instead of dark legs. The Cheveral Goldfinch has a white mark dividing the red below the beak. Both these varieties are rare and highly prized by mule breeders.

Goldfinches will breed as quickly as Canaries, in the aviary or breeding cage; they will also mate with Canaries. To produce the best results, an active male should be placed with a yellow hen canary about the first of May. The male offspring will be magnificent songsters, and of beautiful plumage.

The Goldfinch thrives best on our mixed seed, with occasionally a cupful of maw and lettuce seed, of which it is very fond. They should be kept in cages similar to a canary's. They are very fond of gravel, which should be plentifully strewn in the bottom of the cage.

A young male Goldfinch is worth $2.00, a female, $1.50; a male, when in full song, from $5.00 to $10.00.

Male White-legged or Cheveral Goldfinches, are worth $5.00 each.

THE AMERICAN GOLDFINCH.

The American Goldfinch, or the Yellow Bird, as he is generally called, is found all over our land. He makes one of the most sprightly of cage birds and is readily tamed. The plumage of the male is of a beautiful lemon, with a black cap and lemon and white wings. His song, although not consisting of a very wide range of notes, is sweet and pleasing. Anyone can very easily capture one of these pretty birds by means of limed twigs or a trap cage; the manner of doing so, being fully described in the chapter on trapping birds.

This bird should be treated the same as a Canary, and

THE AMERICAN GOLDFINCH.

kept in the same sort of a cage. An American Goldfinch in fine plumage and accustomed to a cage, is worth $1.50.

THE GREENFINCH.

This bird, known also as the Green Linnet, is about the same size and same shape as the Canary; of yellowish,

green plumage, inclining to gray on the back, and lighter beneath. With age they become yellower. His song, although not of the highest order, is sprightly, and given with great heartiness.

They are robust birds, easily kept in health, and require a cage similar to a Canary's, and thrive under the same foc 1 and treatment. They will interbreed with Canaries, but the mules are neither fine songsters nor of beautiful plumage. The Greenfinch should not be admitted to the aviary, as he is apt to constitute himself a guard over the seed-hopper and attack every bird that approaches it.

A young male Greenfinch is worth $1.50; one in full song, $5.00.

THE LINNET.

The Linnet is one of the nicest of the finch family. He is more grateful for kindness, more solicitous of pleasing, than almost any other cage bird.

During the first year of his life, the Linnet is called a **Gray Linnet**, from the color of his plumage. After the second moult, the red of the breast blending with the amber edges of the feathers, produces a golden hue, and the bird is then known as a Yellow Linnet At the end of the third moult, the breast becomes a bright carmine, and the flanks the color of iron rust, and it is known as the Rose Linnet.

Gray, yellow, or red, his music will be the same; even sickness does not end his exquisite piping; and the older he grows the better he sings

The song of the Linnet cons: of a number of sentences or "jerks," as they are called, and each one distinct from the other, while the wonderful variety of notes is astounding.

He sings both summer and winter, except during the time of shedding feathers. They are very desirable birds for the aviary.

A male Linnet will mate with a female Canary, and the offspring will resemble in color, a gray canary; but the song of the mules will be very fine, and they are highly prized on that account.

Linnets should be kept in a square cage, as in it they are less subject to giddiness than in round cages. They require the same food and management as Canaries.

Young male or female Linnets are worth $1.50; and when in full song, from $5.00 to $10.00.

THE SISKIN.

The Siskin resembles the Goldfinch in shape, although a trifle smaller; the bill is also sharp and pointed. The general color of the plumage of this bird is a yellowish-green on the upper parts of the body, and yellowish-white beneath. The exes of the Siskin are quite easily distinguished, the male bird being brighter, and having a black top to his head; whereas the head of the female is grayish, the body-coloring duller, and the breast spotted. The males increase in brightness of color as they grow older.

They are quite little birds, happy and contented, and with a little attention become very tame. They sing continually in a low, plaintive twitter of much sweetness. Their contented manner and familiar ways cause them to become general favorites of the household into which they are admitted.

The male Siskin is one of the best mimics among the small birds. He will readily catch the notes of all the birds he hears, and mix them up in the drollest fashion, when uttering them as his own.

Siskins require the same general treatment as Canaries, and should be kept in the same kind of cage. They **will** interbreed with Canaries, and the mules are often of handsome plumage and fine singers.

Male or female Siskins are worth $1.50; when in full song, $5.00.

Siskins are sometimes kept in tinned wire cages with wooden backs. The price of such a cage is 75c.

THE BULLFINCH.

There is scarcely another bird as pleasing and engaging in confinement as the Bullfinch. Their pretty plumage, tameness, and winning actions, cause them to be general favorites. Their size is about that of a sparrow; the beak is thickly rounded, and black. The top of the head, wings, and tail are glossy black; the back, bluish gray; and the breast, red. The breast of the female is gray brown.

Their natural song is a soft, low whistle, interspersed with some curious sounds, and accompanied with bowing and waving of the tail, and other grotesque movements.

THE BULLFINCH.

A Bullfinch may early be taught to do wonders; to kiss its owner, to come and go at command, etc. They can be bought already taught to pipe such tunes as "God save the Queen," "Pretty Polly Perkins," and airs from operas. To teach them to whistle these airs requires time and patience, more than the equivalent of the expense of procuring them already taught by poor and patient foreigners. They require the same treatment as the Canary, but a larger cage.

A male Bullfinch will sometimes mate with a female Canary; but mule birds of this kind are hard to raise, and require much time and patience.

If you desire to teach a Bullfinch to pipe, he should be

taken in hand when young, just as soon after he has been imported as possible. Let nobody tend him or supply him with food and water but yourself. Be very particular about that. His music lessons should be given on an empty stomach. Take his seed away from him the day before you begin the lessons, which should be given at day-break. The bird should not hear the least sound except that made by his teacher. If you are capable of whistling clearly and sharply you will need no instrument; but the tune may be played on a tin whistle, a flute, or a flageolet. Play or whistle the first bars over again and again, in exactly the same time; but do not give the little scholar many notes to digest at one time. Fifty times is not too many times to repeat the notes at each lesson. The probabilities are that before the last time the notes are played he will echo them with more or less success. Now for his reward. Fling open the shutters (the lessons should be given in a partially-darkened room), and pile up seed in his cup, and crown the banquet with two or three—just two or three hemp seed. Let that end the lesson. Allow him to eat the seed for a couple of hours and then take it away and do not allow him to eat more that day. The next morning he will commence with the notes in less time than before, and after he is nearly or quite perfect, go on with a few more notes. Reward him the same as before. Continue the lessons until he can pipe the whole tune perfectly and without hesitancy.

If your bird is obstinate, as a punishment you may blow him up, not figuratively, but actually. Walk sharply up to the cage and blow at him with your mouth. He will relish that so little that, after a few applications, a quick step or two towards his cage will be sufficient to put him on his best behavior.

A Bullfinch is worth $3.00; a female, $2.50; one that pipes one tune, $15.00; one that pipes two tunes, $25.00; and one that pipes three tunes, $50.00.

THE INDIGO FINCH.

The Indigo Finch is a beautiful American songster that is deserving of more attention than he has ever received. He is about the size of the Canary, and the plumage is of a most beautiful blue, still more brilliant about the head. He changes his color twice a year turning blue to gray in the

THE INDIGO FINCH.

winter, and changing to blue again in the Spring. The female is gray in color throughout the year.

This Finch has quite an agreeable song which may sometimes be heard even in the middle of the night. They require the same treatment as the Canary, but should occasionally have a little green food, such as chickweed, lettuce, celery, etc. They are very fond of bathing. A cross can be made between a male Indigo Finch and a female Canary. A male Indigo Finch is worth $1.50; in full song, $5.00.

THE CHAFFINCH.

In plumage the Chaffinch is certainly a handsome bird, although the colors are soft and subdued. The head is dark bluish-gray; the back, brown; and the wings, black; the ends of the wing-feathers, white, and bars on the wings. The breast is pinkish-red; the belly inclining to white; the ramp, greenish; the tail, dark. The female is smaller than the male and much duller in plumage.

This bird is a most delightful songster. His short, sharp, clear, thrilling note, is uttered with that earnestness which is so attractive. The Chaffinch, to sing well, should be kept in small cage, a square one being preferable. Feed him on our Mixed Seed, and occasionally give him a meal-worm or some ant eggs. He will breed with a Canary.

THE CHAFFINCH.

Male or female Chaffinches are worth $1.50 ; when in full song, $5.00.

THE RED LINNET.

This bird which is often called the Purple Finch is a beautiful, large, and cheerful songster. The color of the male is

a rich, dark crimson, which is deepest on the upper parts of the body; his tail and wings are of a dusty brown. His song is very sweet, and is sometmes poured forth for hours, with scarcely a minute's intermission for rest He is quite heardy, and will thrive on a diet of canary seed, with occasionally a little sunflower seed, by the way of variety. He will inter-breed with the Canary.

There is no native bird that becomes tame so soon after being captured than this one. He begins to show his appreciation of cage life by beginning to sing after a few weeks of captivity.

A male Red Linnet is worth $2; in full song, $5 00.

THE CROSSBILL.

This is a curious bird, especially noticeable from the

peculiar formation of the beak, from which it derives its name. They are larger and stouter than the Canary. The head is thick, the tail and legs short. They climb about their cage, assisting their movements with their beaks, after the fashion of Parrots.

The Crossbill is subject to great variation of plumage, being sometimes red, and sometimes a greenish yellow. The cage for this bird must be all wire, for it will soon destroy a wooden one. It can be fed upon canary seed and a little hemp with a piece of sweet apple occasionally.

The song of the Crossbill is somewhat harsh. The price of a male bird is $3.00.

THE SERIN FINCH.

This bird is generally known as the St. Helena Canary. It is about the size of a small canary, the beak thick for its length and the plumage of a yellowish green, darker on the upper parts and more inclined to yellow underneath. The female is not so bright in color as the male,

Their neat form, and liveliness the tolerable sweetness and strength of their never-tiring song, cause them to be very desirable cage birds. The males will readily mate with female Canaries. They require the same cage and treatment as the Canary A male Serin Finch is worth $5.00; a female, $3.00

THE SERIN FINCH.

THE CIRIL FINCH.

This bird closely resembles in habits and general appearance a green Canary. It is one of the liveliest and most indefatigable songsters of all cage birds. Its voice, although not strong, is sweet; and, except in a few notes in which it resembles the song of the lark, is remarkably like that of the Canary. It should be kept in a canary cage and will thrive on the same seed that is given to the Canary. In the aviary the Ciril Finch will mate and inter-breed with the canary, goldfinch, linnet, or with the siskin.

THE CIRIL FINCH.

young male Ciril Finch is worth $3.00; when in full song the price is $8.00.

THE NONPAREIL.

This is one of the most beautiful of our American Finches, and has a low, soft, and very agreeable song. He has a violet hood and neck, a red circle around the eyes, and yellowish-green back. The throat, chest, and under part of the body, are of a bright red; and the wings, green. He is rather smaller than the Canary, but requires the same food, cage, and general treatment. He is very fond of bathing, and should be indulged in this cleanly habit.

THE NONPAREIL.

A specimen of the Nonpareil in good plumage, will cost $3.00; when in full song, $5.00.

THE BOBOLINK.

This is a bird that wears a black coat in the spring, with yellow epaulets; and dons a sober suit of russet brown in the autumn. He changes his name with his feathers, for in the spring he is the Bobolink, and later his cognomen is Reedbird. He is a merry songster, and makes an attractive cage bird. He requires a diet of plain canary seed and should be kept in a small-size Mocking Bird cage.

The Bobolink should

THE BOBOLINK.

always be kept on a short allowance of seed, three tablespoonfuls being enough for a day's allowance. He is such a perfect glutton, that if allowed an unlimited supply of seed, he will do but little singing.

With the plumage of the Reedbird he is worth 75c. After he assumes that of the Bobolink, the price increases to $1.50; and when in full song, to $3.00.

THE CARDINAL GROSBEAK, OR RED BIRD.

This is one of the most attractive of our native birds, and is deserving of more attention than has ever been bestowed upon him, as much on account of his brilliant plumage as for his melodious whistling.

He is known by several aliases, among others, the Virginia Nightingale, from his habit of singing in the night, and the Red Bird, from the color of his plumage. In length he is about seven inches. The plumage is of a rich vermillion-red over the entire body, with a darker shade of the same color on wings and tail; the face, cheeks, throat, feet, and legs are black; the bill, red. The head is surmounted with a tuft of brilliant red feathers, which the bird is capable of erecting at will.

The female is of a rich brown, with some red on breast and wings; and, though not so striking in appearance as her husband, is equally as beautiful, and is often as good a whistler.

During the spring months he sings his melody all day long, and often far into the night. There is a great difference in individuals as to musical ability, but no more so than among other birds; as the Mocking-bird, for instance.

The Cardinal Grosbeak is naturally a very active bird; and his cage should be a good sized one, as large as for a Mocking-bird; otherwise he will damage his feathers. Hang him up quite high, so that he may not be needlessly disturbed. The floor of the cage should be strewn with red gravel or silver sand. He will thrive well on canary seed; with unhulled rice and cracked corn, and occasionally a little hemp seed. His drink should be of soft water; hard or lime water having a tendency to make him costive; which, if not cured, will soon carry him off.

Do not keep him too warm, as he is very hardy, enduring the inclemencies of severe winters with great indifference.

The price of a young Cardinal Grosbeak, that is just beginning to whistle, is $3.00. Birds in full song, range from $5.00 to $10.00, according to their proficiency. A suitable cage in walnut and tinned wire, will cost $2.00; in brass the price is $7.50.

THE BRAZILIAN CARDINAL.

This sleek bird, prettily marked gray, white, and black, with crimson head and crest, is sure to have the attention of every beholder. His great activity and his considerable size require a roomy cage, wherein, with fair treatment, he will keep his plumage in perfect condition, entirely indifferent as to the temperature in which he is kept. The song, or rather whistle, of this bird, is loud and clear, and he sings at all seasons of the year except while moulting. The female is of the same beautiful plum-

age as the male, and is equally as good a whistler. Feed upon plain canary seed, with an occasional meal of ant eggs and insects.

A good specimen of the Brazilian Cardinal is worth $5.00; when in full song, $10.00.

THE JAVA SPARROW.

No foreign bird is so generally known as the Java Sparrow. It is rather handsome and especially remarkable for the very perfect condition in which it will always keep its plumage. The soft slate-colored body feathers are always  as close as they can lie, the large white patches on the cheeks are ever clean, the black face and throat skin like new velvet, and the wax-like beak is pink, and looks as if just modeled from wax.

No bird is so easily kept and of so little trouble as the Java Sparrow; it needs only plain canary seed, and can be kept in either a round or square canary cage. Although without song, yet his extreme docility and the ease with which tricks can be taught him, make him a popular cage bird. A pair will breed in a cage as readily as Canaries, and the number of broods they will rear in a year, if permitted, almost surpasses belief.

White Java Sparrows are not, as many suppose, albinos, but a separate variety that are bred by the Japanese, who originated them. Java Sparrows are generally kept in pairs and are worth $4.00 for a male and female; the white variety is sold at $10.00 per pair.

THE HAWFINCH.

This bird is one of the largest of the Finch family. It is about seven inches long and very stoutly made. The general plumage is drab inclining to chestnut on the upper parts and grayer beneath. Most of the tail and large wing

THE HAWFINCH.

feathers are black, having a large white spot on the inner vein. The Hawfinch is very docile, and good tempered in confinement; and the male will pair with a hen Canary.

The song contains some pleasing notes, but their continual cry of "itz, itz," makes them rather unpleasant as cage birds, but they do splendidly in the aviary. They require a diet of canary seed, with oats, buckwheat, or millet as an occasional change.

A male Hawfinch is worth $3.00; a pair of them, $5.00.

TITMICE.

The only variety of Titmice that is kept as pets in this country is the Blue Tit, or Tom Tit, as it is familiarly called. The plumage is very beautiful. The front of the head and the sides are white and a streak of the same extends backwards over the eyes to the nape of the neck. Within this pearly setting is his crown of azure blue. His back is of a bright olive green, the under part of the throat is black; the wings sky blue, tipped with white; and

THE BLUE TIT.

the tail as brilliant as the crown. The female is of more sober plumage than the male.

The Tit is a most active and amusing bird, and is easily tamed. Its song is an indistinct warbling composed of a few strains, with high notes interspersed.

They should be fed on our Mixed Seed, with an occasional meal of ant eggs and meal worms. They are so expert with their bill that they must be kept in an all-metal cage with close wires. A suitable cage in solid brass costs $3.50. These birds are generally sold in pairs, male and female Tits, $8.00. Singly, the male is worth $5.00.

THE WHIDAH BIRD.

This rare and beautiful bird, sometimes wrongly called the Window Finch, is much admired on account of its odd appearance.

Its size is about that of the Canary, but in the male bird two of the feathers of the tail attain the length of thirteen inches. The head, chin, front of the neck, back, wings, and tail are black. The back of the neck is light orange; the breast, upper part of the belly, and thighs are white. In the winter the plumage changes to a dark brown, and the tail feathers are of the ordinary length. The female resembles the male in his winter attire.

These birds are lively and in constant motion, and take

great delight in bathing and keeping their plumage in perfect condition. Their song is rather melancholy and not loud, yet on the whole agreeable. They are very hardy, and thrive on canary seed alone; but a little occasional green food is beneficial. They must be kept in a high cage or their tail will get worn off. For the aviary they are among the most showy birds that can be selected.

A male Whidah bird in perfect plumage is worth $8; a female, $4.

THE WEAVER BIRD.

This is one of the most interesting families of foreign cage birds. Kept in an aviary, where they will display their wonderful ingenuity in nest building, no more amusing pets can be found. Even in a roomy cage, in which a few branches and a quantity of stiff fibre has been placed, the male of a pair of Weaver Birds will, without delay, begin to build nest after nest, probably pulling most of them to pieces, when half finished, if their construction does not entirely please the proud architect. There are many varieties of these curious birds, the most common of which is in general color a dull yellow blotched with brown;

THE WEAVER BIRD.

the throat being black. It suspends a skillfully-woven nest, in the shape of an inverted flask, the entrance being at the extremity of a prolonged neck, through which is the passage to a snug little chamber in the round body of the nest itself. This variety of Weaver Bird is worth $6.00 per pair. Other birds, of more resplendent plumage, vary from $8.00 to $25.00 per pair.

RED-WINGED BLACKBIRD.

This is a very handsome bird, the male of which is glossy black all over, with the exception of the shoulders, which are yellow and red. The female is of a sober gray.

The male has a clear, cheery note; and makes a most excellent and very attractive cage bird. In confinement they thrive on a diet of canary seed. Like the Bobolink, they will get too fat if the amount fed to them is not restricted to three tablespoonfuls a day.

They require a small size Mocking Bird cage, and in addition to seed should have an occasional meal of Mocking Bird Food and ant-eggs.

A male Red-winged Blackbird is worth $1.50; in full song, $3.00.

THE YELLOWHAMMER.

The plumage of the male Yellowhammer is certainly attractive. The head and throat are of a clear, bright, pale yellow, and the general plumage of the body is an olive brown. The young males are of a yellowish-gray, until a year old; and the females are always of this color.

THE YELLOWHAMMER.

They are very good singers, and make nice cage birds. In size they are somewhat larger than the Canary. They will eat canary seed, oats, and other seeds; but their diet should be varied often by feeding them on hard-boiled eggs, ant eggs, and meal worms. They are very fond of insects and will greedily catch and eat every fly that gets within their reach.

A male Yellowhammer is worth $2.50.

THE ROSE-BREASTED GROSBEAK.

This magnificent bird is very little known, yet few birds surpass him in brilliancy of plumage or sweetness of song. Night, as well as day, he pipes his merry notes, which are clear and mellow. He has a bright carmine breast, and a body part white, part black. He requires a diet of canary seed, and a small-sized Mocking Bird cage. A good specimen of this bird is worth $5.00.

Very hardy, he will stand almost any degree of cold; while if kept in a hot room his song soon fails, and he sits on his perch, dumpy and unhappy.

THE CITRIL FINCH.

This bird is also closely allied to the Canary, and is often called the Italian Canary. By some writers it is supposed that the domestic Canary first originated by crossing the wild Canary with the Finch. In form and color it closely resembles the common Canary, except that it is rather slighter in build. The plumage is very beautiful, and the song resembles that of the Canary, only it is not so shrill, but more flute-like. They will breed readily in the aviary, and the males will inter-breed with female Canaries. It is perhaps unnecessary to add, that the same general treatment is required as for Canaries.

The male Citril Finch is worth $5.00; the female, $3.00.

THE BOHEMIAN WAXWING.

This bird, also known as the Cedar Bird, is of very beautiful soft-colored plumage, and has a singular appendage to the wings, bearing a striking resemblance to a drop of red sealing-wax. Its note is not unlike that of the Thrush, but is more uncertain and weaker. While singing it agitates the crest on its head. It requires a Mocking Bird cage, which should not be kept in too warm a room, as it is a very hardy bird and likes cold weather. It requires Prepared Mocking Bird Food. A male specimen of the Bohemian Waxwing, in good plumage will cost $3.00.

AFRICAN FINCHES.

These diminutive Finches vary in size from that of a Canary down to almost the smallness of a humming bird. They are always kept in pairs, and they spend much of their time in caressing and arranging each others feathers. They are fed upon maw, canary, and millet seed; and require a cage with close wires, as they can easily escape through the bars of an ordinary canary cage.

THE NUTMEG FINCH.

The room in which they are kept should never be below 60° in winter. Many of the varieties will breed in a cage or in the aviary.

It is usual to keep a collection of from six

THE AVADAVAT.

THE WAXBILL.

to fifty in one cage. We furnish a walnut cage suitable for six pairs of these birds for $1.00; one of brass that will comfortably accommodate four pairs, $3.25. It would be useless to enumerate all of these brilliant-hued birds, as there are hundreds of different kinds; so only the varieties most frequently met with are described.

THE CHESTNUT FINCH, or NUTMEG BIRD, is very curiously marked, rich chocolate on the back, and with numerous white crescents on the lower body. By no means delicate, these birds will live for years in a cage or an aviary, and they will not require very particular care.

THE AVADAVAT is one of the smallest of Finches, and is vivacious and graceful in his movements. His plumage is dark brown, with a carmine tint, and covered all

THE ZEBRA.

over with small pearl-white spots; the beak is coral-red. The female is more soberly attired. Both sexes have a sweet, melodious song. They will breed in an aviary or cage, if supplied with the proper accommodations. The breeding season with them begins about Christmas.

THE WAXBILL has a grayish-brown plumage, marked with extremely faint wave-like dark lines athwart the body. The abdomen is of a very bright roseate hue, which is brightest in the centre,

THE SILVERBEAK.

and fainter towards the sides and chest. The beak is red. When the bird sings, the tail is extended to a fan shape. Male and female are alike, and both are equally active and cheerful, and among the hardiest of the Finches. There are several varieties of the Waxbill, which differ in minor points.

WHITE-HEADED NUN.

THE WANAKIN.

THE ZEBRA is very small in size, and his plumage is a dark greenish-brown on the back; the throat, chest, and lower body are pale yellow, with a diffused patch of bright orange about the middle of the lower part of the body. The beak is red, and a red line extends from the beak through the eye towards the ear. The female is without the orange on the lower part of the body. They make most bright and intelligent pets.

THE SILVERBEAK is exceedingly amiable in the aviary, and very easily kept, bred, and reared. The upper part of the body is fawn; the wings and tail, a shade darker; and the lower part of the body, white; the beak is silver-gray. The male constantly sings a pleasing little song.

THE WHITE-HEADED NUN, or Meja Finch, is of a soft chestnut-brown all over, except the head, which is a silver-gray, delicately shaded where the neck joins the shoulders.

THE CUT-THROAT.

THE BLACK-HEADED NUN is of a bright rich chestnut brown; the head, neck, and upper part of the breast being deep black.

THE CUT-THROAT has a red band extending from ear to ear across the throat. The female is without this band. The soft fawn color and delicate markings of the rest of the plumage are remarkably pretty. They will readily breed in a cage.

DIAMOND SPARROW.

THE DIAMOND SPARROW's head and back are silver-gray; the wings and tail darker gray; the breast and lower part of the body chestnut, ornamented with irregular white spots; the chest is crossed by a band of velvet black; and the end of the back and root of the tail is of a rich crimson.

THE MAGPIE FINCH, or Bronze Wanakin is of a glossy black, with tinges of purple and violet on the head, throat, wings, and back; on the breast he is pure white. He is very playful, and will mate and breed readily.

THE ORANGE CHEEK.

THE ORANGE CHEEK WAXBILL has quite a pleasant song. In color he is mainly of a light grayish brown, with orange spots on his cheeks, from which he derives his name. On the abdomen there is also a patch of orange; the tail is dark brown, with a crimson root. The beak is coral red.

THE CORDON-BLEU is one of the showiest of Finches, and is a sprightly singer. The plumage is pale brownish gray on the back; the face, throat, chest, and tail of pale sky blue. The cheeks of the male are ornamented with crimson patches.

The prices of African Finches vary from $4.00 to $10.00 per pair, according to the variety.

THE CORDON-BLEU.

THE FIRE FINCH is of dark red
plumage, except the back and tail,
which are dark greenish-brown. On
the sides there are a few minute spots,
which, however, are frequently absent
in young birds. The beak is coral-
red, and around the eye is a narrow,
straw-colored ring. The female is
dark brown, with a little red at the
root of the tail, and the same tiny
white spots on the sides. They will
readily build a nest, provided they
feel at home, and the climate is hot
enough to remind them of Central
Africa.

THE MAGPIE FINCH.

THE CINDER FINCH is of delicate
soft lavender or pale slate, all over the body. The lower
part of the body and the tail are purple, and the beak crimson. A line of black runs from the beak beyond the eye.
They will breed freely.

THE MOCKING BIRD.

We should take especial pride in the mocking bird; for
it is a bird peculiar to the American continent. Its torrent
of mimicry pours upon us the songs of a dozen different
birds ; and many of the cries heard in the barnyard. This
unique songster unites in itself more excellencies than any
other bird possesses. Spring, summer, and autumn, its
harmonious and varied song thrills and holds spell-bound
the listener. The pipe of the canary ; the mellow whistle
of the cardinal; the wild song of the thrush; the shrill
scream of the eagle; the exquisite warble of the bluebird ;
the mourning of the dove; the cock's crow; the hen's
cackle; the cry of the katydid ; the grunt of the pig; and
the infernal noise of quarreling cats :—all this medley issues
in rapid succession from that master-mimic, the Mocking
Bird! No wonder that it is a general favorite.

The Mocking Bird is not showy in appearance, but its
well-shaped form and lively and graceful motions make it
an attractive household pet, apart from its song. It measures nine-and-a-half inches in length ; and at an expanse of

wings, thirteen inches. The upper part of the head, neck, and back is dark brownish-ash; the wings and tail are nearly black; the primary feathers are white, the first and second row of coverts, tipped with white. The tail is cuneiform; the two outer feathers are wholly white, the others, except the middle ones, tipped with white. The neck, breast, and whole under parts, clouded white. The iris is of a yellowish cream color. The bill is black; and the base of the lower mandible, whitish. The legs and feet are black, and stoutly formed.

The male and female Mocking Bird are very similar in plumage; but they may be readily distinguished by no-

THE MOCKING BIRD.

ticing the following differences; The white on the wings of the male bird extends over the whole nine primaries, or quill feathers, down to and well over the coverts; these are also white, though sometimes tipped with brown; the white of the primaries extending equally on both vanes of the feather. In the female the white is not so clear, and extends only over seven or eight of the primaries; the black of the wing is also less deep, being of a brownish shade.

Occasionally males are met with that are wonderful songsters, and yet are very poorly marked according to the standard we have given; but in buying young birds it is always better to secure the best marked birds; as they are sure to be males.

To rear the young of the Mocking Bird by hand successfully, regularity of feeding and cleanliness are of the greatest importance. To keep them growing steadily they should be fed very often, and not much at a time. They should be fed long after they need assistance; as that keeps them strong, while rendering them more gentle and confiding.

The cage for a Mocking Bird should be large, and kept very clean; and should be supplied with plenty of gravel.

One of the cheapest and most desirable styles of cages for these birds is made of walnut, with polished iron wire. It is 18 inches high, but is in three lengths, as follows: 22 inches long, $1.75; 28 inches long, $2.50; 30 inches long, $3.00. The cups for this cage cost 25 cents, extra. We illustrate a cage of brass wire, with black walnut base. It is also made in three sizes: 18 inches, $8.50; 22 inches, $13 00; 26 inches, $15.00. A bath dish for a Mocking Bird is worth 25 cents.

The bird must never be exposed to inclement weather; but should have the benefit of fresh air as much as possible; protected, however, from the scorching rays of the sun by a covering thrown over the cage.

The bill of fare best suited to the Mocking Bird will be found on page 10, under the head of "Soft-Billed Birds." They are fond of boiled carrot or beet root mashed and squeezed dry. Boiled cabbage, cauliflower, and peas are good for them; also a very little roast meat minced, and a little of the hard-boiled yolk of an egg. They like ripe pears, elder-berries, currants, and cherries. A few ant eggs soaked and mixed with the food is very beneficial. A little sweet apple grated up with the food gives it a fine flavor, and often restores the appetite when it is poor, during hot weather or when moulting. Our Prepared Mocking Bird Food, mixed with one-quarter grated carrot, is perhaps the best for a steady diet. The Mocking Bird is omnivorous, feeding on berries, insects, and fruit. For this reason a supply of insects should be gathered during the proper season; such as flies, grasshoppers, spiders, and the like; and put loosely in a paper bag, and hung up to dry.

When used in winter, they should have boiling water poured over them, which will soften them, and make them fully as palatable as if they were still alive. Another dainty morsel is currants that have been washed clean, soaked over night, and then wiped thoroughly dry.

But the richest of food is meal-worms. Six to ten worms a month, are sufficient to make the bird lively. It is a good plan to raise a stock of these worms. The process is quite simple, and has been fully explained on a previous page.

Nine-tenths of the ailments of the Mocking-Bird is caused by improper feeding, and the use of inferior prepared foods. Green food given daily, grapes, meat from the table, sugar, and candy, are all bad for the bird. It needs a plain, but varied diet, and to be fed and watered at the same time every day. A bath should be given daily; and the vessel removed from the cage when the bird has bathed. During May, often earlier, some Mocking Birds have the mating fever; they grow melancholy, allow their feathers to become rough, cease to p'ume themselves before retiring, waste away, and die. In many cases they forget this inclination for freedom and a mate, by simply changing the cage; hanging it near a window, where the r time will be taken up in watching new surroundings. Should the bird's feathe s stand loosely all over, and he still seem healthy, give him cooling food only. Should the bird be dumpish and stupid, a few spiders will sometimes cure him. Should he refuse to eat, examine his tongue, and if a horny scale is seen upon it, this must be removed with great care; for if it is allowed to remain the bird will surely die. To remove this scale, h ld the bird on his back firmly with one hand, while with the finger-nail of the other hand, gently peel it from the tongue, and anoint with honey and borax.

Mites are a great annoyance to a bird, and should be got rid of by using our Mite Exterminator, according to directions.

For blindness there is no remedy, for it is only a symptom of disease of the brain and that is always fatal; it is almost invariably caused by the use of inferior prepared food, in which there is an excess of hemp or maw meal. Baldness, or dropping of the head feathers, is generally fatal. It usually commences around the eyes, and the symptoms preceding its appearance are continued restlessness and rubbing of the parts on the perch or cage. It may be **treated** with flower of sulphur, rubbed up with a little water to the consistency of paste, and applied twice a day to the affected parts. This will allay the itching, and if early applied, may check the disease.

In doctoring the sick bird, ascertain as nearly as possible what the complaint is, by comparing the symptoms with the printed ones accompanying our *Bird Bitters*, and treat the patient according to directions.

Nearly all Mocking Birds are bought when young by their owners, because old ones in perfect song, bring such high prices, even as much as $50 has been refused for a very fine bird. It should be borne in mind when buying these youngsters, that birds taken from the nest and fed by hand are much superior to ones that are trapped after they leave the nest. The former become very tame, while the latter nearly always remain wild and flutter about the cage when it is approached. The farther south the birds come from the finer songsters they make. Young birds begin to arrive about the latter part of August. From then until October 1, we offer hand-fed Florida Mocking Birds, guaranteed males, $5.00 each; trapped North Carolina birds, guaranteed males, $3.00. Mocking Birds just commencing to whistle, $10.00. Birds in full song, $10.00 to $15.00 according to their ability.

THE REDSTART.

The beautiful plumage of this bird would alone recommend it to special notice. However, besides his handsome feathers, he possesses a good temper, an active disposition and a pleasing song.

He is about the size of a Canary. The sides of the head are black; the throat speckled with white; the back and belly a mixture of lurid red and gray; the wings are dark brown, and the tail is red.

The Redstart requires the same style of cage and the same general treatment as the B'ack Cap.

A good specimen of a young male Redstart is worth $5.00; in full song, $10.00.

THE NIGHTINGALE.

We now come to the bird about which more poetry has been written than any other feathered songster. When everyone is asleep, his tiny throat pours forth its sweet music to the moon; but when caged he sings by day and night, and his is the music that one never wishes still. In plumage he is a modest bird, and in size he is about as large as a blue bird.

It has always been a matter of surprise that such a small bird as the Nightingale should possess such wonderful song-power, as its singing can be heard, on a still night, at a distance of a mile; but the fact is explained by the great strength of the muscles of the throat.

The Nightingale requires a large cage, which should be hung in a subdued light. A cage with the back and sides of dark wood, is the best for this bird, and the roof should be covered, on the inside, with green baize, thus preventing the bird's head from being injured when he flies upward. The perches should be covered with soft material, as his feet are very tender, and apt to become sore when plain wooden perches are used. The cost of such a cage is $3.50. The same treatment is required as for other soft-billed birds. Although apt to be rather a delicate bird when first caught, after once becoming accustomed to cage life, it is among the longest-lived of cage birds, instances being known of Nightingales having lived fourteen years in confinement.

A Nightingale beginning to sing is worth $15.00; in full song, from $25.00 to $50.00.

THE ENGLISH THRUSH.

The English Thrush is one of the finest of soft-billed songsters. His sweet and merry song makes all rejoice who hear it. In size he is about as large as our Robin, and is speckled yellow, which is the color of its bill. Thrushes possess imitative powers in a marvelous degree, tunes played or whistled to them are readily acquired. They require the same treatment and cage as Mocking Birds. The snails that are found in ponds and rivers make them a treat of which they are passionately fond. It is worth the trouble of collecting these, to see them break the shells against the wires or perches of the cage. There are several varieties of Thrushes, but the one most commonly imported to this country is the Song Thrush mentioned above.

THE ENGLISH THRUSH.

A young Thrush coming into song, is worth $8.00; in full song, from $10.00 to $25.00.

THE BLACK CAP.

It is no uncommon thing for the song of the Black Cap to be spoken of as rivaling that of the nightingale, and some writers go so far as to assert that between the melody of the two it is next to impossible to distinguish. This bird is smaller than the Canary, and has a plumage of olive

THE BLACK CAP.

green and gray, with a dingy white throat, and a black cap on the head.

It is a soft-billed bird, and requires to be fed upon our Prepared Mocking Bird Food. It requires an oblong cage of small size, with a tin wool, is worth $1.25, and in brass $5.50. A Black Cap, coming into song, will cost $5.00; after the song is perfected, $10.00.

THE ENGLISH BLACKBIRD.

The English Blackbird is a jovial, jolly fellow; with a fine, hearty, and mellow whistle that grows louder during rainy weather. In size and build he somewhat resembles our Robin. He will learn to pipe any easy tune that is whistled to him. When once learned he will never forget it. He is jet black, with a yellow bill. He requires the general treatment given to all the soft-billed birds, and should be kept in a mockingbird cage of large size.

An English Blackbird, beginning to whistle, is worth $6.00; in full song, $10.00.

English Blackbirds are very hardy, and soon become so tame that they can be taken out of the cage, and will whistle lustily while perched on their owner's finger. They will breed in an aviary. They are fond of bathing, and water for this purpose should be supplied daily.

THE ENGLISH ROBIN.

THE ENGLISH ROBIN.

The Redbreast, which is the national bird of England, is smaller than our Robin, resembling the latter only by the red on the breast. As a cage bird, he is very gentle, lively, and affectionate; and sings his merry song summer and winter, often far into the night.

The treatment given in the first part of this book for soft-billed birds is applicable also to the English Robin. He should be kept in an oblong cage. An English Robin is worth $5.00; when in full song, $10.00.

THE JAPANESE ROBIN.

This is one of the most active and merry of cage birds. He is always hopping from perch to perch, not stopping to sing, but pouring forth his merry song as he goes. In size he is about as large as an English Robin. The back is olive brown, changing to yellow at the head, and to gray on the sides. The throat and breast have a patch of bright orange, shaded towards the border. The wings are dark, each wing-feather edged with orange. The beak and feet are bright coral red. A small size Mocking-Bird cage and soft food are required for their proper comfort. A young male Japanese Robin is worth $5.00; when in full song, $10.00.

THE MAGPIE.

Although without song, Magpies make most amusing pets; and instances of their learning to repeat words and sentences are not rare. He is about the size of our crow, and the plumage is of white and a purple-tinted black. He is more readily tamed than almost any other bird, and requires very little care, as he may be fed upon scraps from the table. Being a large bird he requires a roomy cage, and should be frequently allowed the liberty of a room; where his quaint ways and funny tricks are most amusing. He should never be kept in an aviary with other birds, as he is very likely to destroy the nests, and eat the eggs and young birds; and, in fact, in a short time, play sad havoc with the entire aviary. A young Magpie is worth $5.00.

THE MAGPIE.

THE MINO.

THE MINO.

The Mino, sometimes called the Mynah, is a member of the Starling family.

He is the talking cage-bird of India and China, and possesses power of song with a talent for imitating the human voice. He is a little larger than a European Starling, and much stouter. The plumage is black, with a white bar on the wings; the feet and rather short beak are yellow, and a ring of the same tint surrounds the eye. There are yellow patches on the side of the head, and collar-like appendages of bare orange-colored skin extend from the ears downward.

These birds can be fed upon Mocking Bird Food, but will eat almost anything. Small pieces of raw beef, plenty of ripe fruit, and a little boiled rice, are very good additions to their diet.

A young Mino is worth from $10.00 to $50.00; one that talks is valued at almost any price from $50.00 upwards.

THE BLUE JAY.

The American Blue Jay is a handsome bird, and an unequaled mimic. He will with equal facility imitate the softest sounds and the harshest sounds, but seems to delight more in the loud noises that he hears about him, such as the whining of a dog, the crying of a baby, etc. On his head he wears a light blue crest, which he can elevate at pleasure; the rest of him is of blue in various shades. He is very docile in confinement and can easily be taught innumerable tricks.

As to diet, he should be fed principally on cracked corn, with shreds of lean meat and an occasional meal worm. He is very fond of raw egg; he will puncture the shell with his bill, and then suck the contents. A very large cage is necessary for the proper comfort of the Jay.

A male bird in good plumage, is worth $5.00.

EUROPEAN JAY.

This bird is rather larger than our Jay and is not of so gaudy plumage: which is a purplish gray, with a black stripe running from the beak to the middle of the neck.

The wings are crossed by bright, narrow stripes of blue; the tail is black.

The docility of the European Jay is its chief recommendation as a cage bird. It can be taught to speak, to whistle airs and imitate various noises and the songs of other birds.

It will thrive on a diet of canary seed and wheat, with occasionally a few shreds of raw meat.

It requires a large mocking bird cage. For the aviary it is not desirable, as it is apt to be rather mischievous and delights in tearing the nests of the other birds to pieces, sucking the eggs or devouring the nestlings.

A male European Jay is worth $7.00; when trained, $15.00 to $50.00.

THE RAVEN.

The European Raven makes a most amusing pet; and his tricks, though mischievous, are very laughable. He is considerably larger than a crow, but has the same glossy black plumage as the latter. If kept in a cage, a very strong one is necessary, such as is used for parrots; and he can be chained to a perch the same as the latter.

There is scarcely anything that can be given him which he will not eat and thrive upon: grain, meat, or vegetables, There are many well authenticated instances where Ravens have been taught to talk.

A Raven is worth $5.00.

THE CAT BIRD.

This quaint and delightful native songster is of the same family as the Mocking Bird; and is very similar in habits, requiring the same treatment and cage.

It is a wonder why his musical abilities have not been more fully appreciated; but we suppose it is his sober color and the scolding, cat-like call with which at certain seasons of the year he is apt to greet all who stumble across his nest. In confinement this curious noise is abandoned for more musical notes.

A young male Cat Bird is worth $3.00; when in full song, $5.00.

THE SKYLARK.

The song of the Skylark is considered by some persons to be superior even to that of the Nightingale. It is a bird of modest plumage but trim and neat. The male can be distinguished from the female by the breast of the latter being nearly white. This bird should be fed upon our Prepared Mocking Bird Food, with an occasional meal of seed. The cage in which the Skylark should be kept, as shown in the engraving differs from the shape of other cages, by having a bow window. This is for the reception of a piece of fresh sod, which should be given at least three times a week. Here the lark will stand and sing his musical thanks until his little throat almost bursts. There are no perches in the cage, as the bird will always stay on the bottom. Such a cage will cost $3.50. The price of a young male Skylark is $5.00; when in full song, $10.00. Extra fine singers are sometimes worth $50.00 to $100.00.

THE SKYLARK.

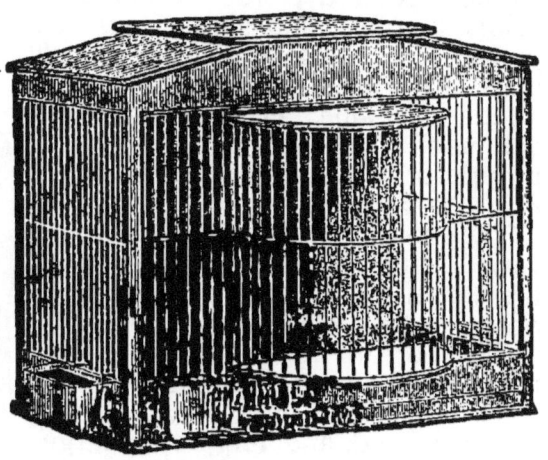

CAGE FOR LARK.

THE WOODLARK.

The song of the Woodlark is considered by many to be fully equal to that of the Skylark, whom he much resembles in plumage, although he is smaller and has a shorter tail. He should be kept in the same kind of a cage as a Skylark, and he requires the same treatment. The price for a good specimen of this bird is about the same as for the Skylark.

THE BALTIMORE ORIOLE.

This bird, which is also known as the Hanging Bird, Swing Bird, and Golden Robin, is of brilliant orange and glistening black plumage, with a few stripes of black upon the wing. From these he derived his name, as they were the colors of Lord Baltimore, the first proprietor of Maryland. The female is of a sober hue.

The song of this bird is loud, varied, and entertaining; and strikes the ear of the listener more like the notes of the fife mingled with the mellow breathing of the flute, than the song of a feathered musician.

He will thrive on a diet of Mocking Bird Food, and requires a large, roomy cage.

A good specimen of a young male Baltimore Oriole is worth $3.00; when in full song, $10.00.

BALTIMORE ORIOLE.

THE TROPIAL.

The Tropial is a South American bird, about the size of our Robin, and has beautiful orange and black plumage. He is almost as good a mimic as the Mocking Bird; and his natural song is clear, flute-like, and powerful; and is sent forth almost continually from morning until night. When young they may be readily taught to whistle airs by frequently playing them on a flageolet or flute in their hearing.

They are extremely active and graceful, and soon become familiar with their owners, and very much attached to them. They should be fed upon our Prepared Mocking Bird Food. Any cage suitable for a Mocking Bird will do for them, and their general treatment is the same.

More of these birds are kept as cage pets in this country than perhaps any other songster, except the Mocking Bird; and they well deserve their great popularity.

A young Tropial is worth $8.00; in full song, $12.00. It is perhaps more satisfactory to purchase a young bird; as it will become more tame. Male birds always prove to be excellent whistlers.

THE STARLING.

The Starling is one of the most gifted of birds. His sagacity is wonderful — he can sing, whistle, and talk. The last accomplishment can be taught to him almost as readily as to a Parrot. In size, he is larger than a cow Blackbird, and is of a lustrous greenish-black, with greenish speckles over the body; the bill is brown.

Starlings require a large size Mocking Bird cage, and should be fed upon Prepared Mocking Bird Food.

A male Starling, beginning to whistle, is worth $5.00; one that talks, $25.00 to $100.00.

THE JACKDAW.

In confinement the Jackdaw becomes thoroughly domesticated, and can be allowed his full liberty, speedily becoming as tame as any inhabitant of the poultry yard. He can be taught to repeat words almost as readily as the parrot, although his capabilities in this respect are not so great. He is as full of mischief as a child, and just as petulant when thwarted in his schemes. He is not as large as a raven, measuring 14 inches when full grown. No special treatment is required, as he will eat anything and everything.

A Jackdaw is worth $5.00.

THE BLUE BIRD.

THE BLUE BIRD.

Everyone knows the plumage and song of the Blue Bird, so it would be useless to spare the space for a detailed description of this bird.

In Europe the Blue Bird is kept as a cage bird, and he is much admired for both his song and plumage, where he is usually called the Blue Robin.

He requires a mixed diet of our Prepared Mocking Bird food and Canary seed.

The price of a Blue Bird in good plumage is $1.00.

THE SWAMP ROBIN.

This breed, which is also known in different parts of the country under several aliases, is really a Thrush, and one of the handsomest-feathered of the family. He is about the size of a Bobolink, is of striking plumage, and a most excellent songster. A small-size Mocking-Bird cage is required for his comfort, and the same treatment as for other birds of the Thrush family.

THE SWAMP ROBIN.

A young male Swamp Robin is worth $3.00; when in full song, $10.00.

THE AMERICAN ROBIN.

Our own Robin, or, properly, the migratory Thrush, makes a most delightful cage bird, whose whistle is not inferior to that of the English Blackbird, which it much resembles. He will readily pick up tunes that are frequently whistled to him. He requires the same general treatment that applies to all soft-billed birds

AMERICAN ROBIN.

When taken from the nest to rear by hand nothing is better to feed them with than the yolk of hard-boiled egg, and corn meal boiled with milk.

A male bird that whistles is worth from $3.00 to $10.00; a young male, $2.00.

THE CROW.

Our native Crow is a very wise bird, and when kept as a pet, is a source of constant amusement and astonishment at his capability. We have come across several specimens that could repeat words, and one that spoke whole sentences. He can be kept either in a parrot cage or chained to a perch. He will become very tame and fearless; and may, after he has been in captivity for some time, be allowed occasional liberty, without fear of his flying far away.

The same general treatment is required as for the Raven. A Crow is worth $2.50.

THE AMERICAN THRUSH.

The large native Brown Thrush, or Thrasher, is believed by all true Americans to surpass in sweetness and variety of song the celebrated Throstle or Mavis of England; and indeed he is scarcely inferior to our own Mocking Bird in voice and talent. He is another of the choice but neglected songsters of our native land.

His song is loud, bold, striking, and full of originality, and given at all hours of the day and night, but most frequently in the morning. He becomes very amusing and sociable in confinement, and shows the warmest attachment for the person who attends to his wants. He should be kept warm in the winter, and requires the same cage and treatment as his cousin, the Mocking Bird.

THE HERMIT THRUSH.

A young male American Thrush is worth $5.00; when in full song, $10.00.

THE SCARLET TANAGER.

The Scarlet Tanager is one of the most beautiful of cage birds, and it is difficult to imagine a plumage more exquisite than his glittering coat of bright scarlet and deep ebony. The young are at first of a greenish olive, but acquire the beautifully contrasting plumage of scarlet and black, when a year old.

The song of the male, which he will deliver for hours together, is a sweet, mellow, and harmonious ditty, of consid-

erable strength and power. He has some notes which are wonderfully soft and flute-like.

The diet required for this bird is canary seed, with a frequent addition of boiled egg, dried cherries, figs, raisins, currants, and meal worms.

A male Scarlet Tanager is worth $3.50; in full song, $5 to $10.00.

THE REDPOLL.

In color and markings the Redpoll somewhat resembles the Linnet; but in shape, size, and habits it is more like the Siskin. It derives its name from the red spot on the top of the head or poll. Like the Linnet, they lose the fine color at their first moult in confinement, and assume a yellowish garb.

The Redpoll is a very intelligent bird; and its song is a low, continuous twittering. He may be taught to draw off his own water, to eat out of the hand, and similar feats. The male and female will pair and breed in a cage or in the aviary; and will also interbreed with the Canary.

Male or female Redpolls are worth $3.00 each or $5.00 per pair.

RING DOVES.

RING DOVE.

Ring Doves, or Mourning Doves, as they are sometimes called, from the peculiar sound they make, are very pretty pets. Their plumage is very sleek, of a yellowish dun color, with a black ring about the neck.

They become very tame and can be readily handled. They breed even more prolifically than pigeons, laying two white eggs; and the male bird taking care of the nestlings while the female builds another nest and lays again.

They require the largest size of a canary-breeding cage (worth $3.50), and should be fed on cracked corn and wheat. They will also eat canary seed.

These birds often throw White, or Albino Doves, that are very beautiful. A pair of Ring Doves are worth $2.00; Albino Doves, $10.00 per pair.

THE CALIFORNIA QUAIL.

This is by far the handsomest member of the Quail family. It is called the Plumed Partridge, because it has a crest or crown of six long feathers on the head. The female is somewhat more soberly attired than the male. In confinement they soon become thoroughly domesticated, and will breed, in a large cage; but more readily in an aviary or large pen built out of doors.

Price per pair, $10.00, for either the mountain or valley variety.

THE EUROPEAN QUAIL.

The European, or Migratory Quail, are somewhat smaller than their American cousins. They will thrive equally well in a large cage or in the aviary, and will build their nest and rear their young in either. They become very tame and much attached to the person feeding them. Like all of the Quail family they require, in confinement, a diet of mixed buckwheat and wheat, with occasional grains of hemp seed.

European Quail are worth $5.00 per pair.

THE AMERICAN QUAIL.

The American Quail, or Bob White, as he is familiarly called by every school-boy in the United States, will breed readily in an aviary or enclosure, but will not do well in a cage. His loud, cheerful whistle, is quite attractive; and his quaint, sociable ways, make him a most interesting pet

Quail are worth, per pair, $2.50.

After the first snow we can always furnish live Quail, at very reasonable figures, by the hundreds, to stock gunning districts. The price of Quail in quantities is, necessarily, a matter of correspondence, and will vary greatly according to the season. Some years they are plentiful, and consequently cheap; while at other times they are scarce, and of course high in price.

PARRAKEETS.

The various species of Parrakeets differ much in size; some being no larger than a sparrow; others being about the size of a Cuban Parrot. All require a diet of plain canary seed, with occasionally a little unhulled rice. The smaller kinds can be kept in any kind of a canary cage, but we advise a square cage of solid brass, with a sliding bottom The cost of such a cage is $5.50. Larger species require a special cage, the best styles of which are illustrated near the end of this book.

Nearly all the different species of Parrakeets breed readily in confinement, either in a large roomy cage or in an **aviary.**

The kind of a nest box required is described under the heading, "The indoor Aviary," in the earlier part of the book.

THE AUSTRALIAN PARRAKEET.

This species is the most popular of small Parrakeets. They are about the size of a Canary, but their long tail makes them appear much larger. The plumage is a beautiful green on the breast and tail, and green dappled with yellow on the back and wings, and shading to yellow on the head. The sexes are very similar. They will breed freely in confinement, and require for a nest a cocoanut shell, with a hole bored in it, and the meat extracted. With this curious nest in an ordinary breeding cage, these birds will set-up house-keeping, when the proper season commences; and raise several broods of young ones. Nearly all the Parrakeets that are brought to this country are cage-bred in Europe. Australian Parrakeets require no other seed excepting plain Sicily canary.

It requires but very little time or patience to tame a pair of these birds, so that they will jump on your finger, come when called, and other pleasing little tricks.

They can be allowed to range around a room at will, and may be depended upon to return to their cage at night. When allowed their liberty in this way, they soon are on familiar terms with their owner. A pair is worth $7.00.

CUT-THROAT COCKATOO.

The Cut-throat Cockatoo is a very curious member of the Parrot family. It has a snow-white plumage with a red streak on its throat, from which it gets its name. The upper mandible is much longer than the lower; and the beak, unlike that of most Parrots, is quite slender. It does not make a very good talker, but is kept as a cage bird on account of its odd appearance.

THE COCKATEEL.

The sober-colored Cockateel is the most gentle and amiable of all Parrakeets, and is about the size of a common pigeon.

He is of a dun color, with lemon cheeks, and a spot of red on them; and a gay crest on his head. Never noisy and not destructive, a pair of these birds may be kept in a roomy cage in any sitting-room, and can be safely associated in an aviary with the smallest of Finches. Few birds breed more readily in captivity; they lay from one to two eggs, which are hatched in about three weeks. A small box with a small hole at one end should be placed in the cage for them to nest in.

He is very frugal in his food, which should consist of canary and a little millet seed; but when breeding a soft food made of stale bread and scalded milk with a little oat-meal, should be given. Cockateels will sometimes learn to talk.

A pair of good specimens is worth $10.00.

THE MARICABO PARRAKEETS.

This Parrakeet is about the same size as the preceding variety, but in color is green, with orange cheeks and forehead. They can be taught to talk, and make very tame and affectionate pets. They are worth $12.00 per pair.

THE AFRICAN LOVE BIRD.

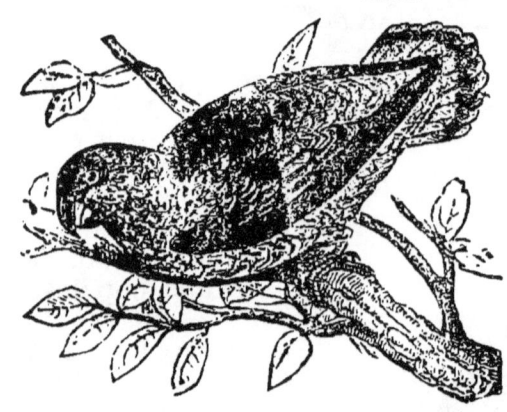

AFRICAN LOVE BIRD.

The African Love Bird, is of a bright green color, and about as large as the preceding species, but have short tails. Some have red faces, others are all green. They are always sold in pairs, and are very affectionate, spending most of their time caressing each other. They can be easily taught to sit on the finger and to kiss their owner, and can be allowed to fly about a room. They are worth $6.00 per pair.

THE QUAKER LOVE BIRD

is similar to the above, but the head and shoulders are of a modest dun color, the rest of the body being bright green. They require the same treatment and cage as the other varieties. They also are worth $6.00 per pair.

HOW WE SELL PARROTS.

We send out nothing but good, healthy specimens and in the case of young birds give a guarantee that it will talk inside of ninety days from the time it is purchased, or we will exchange for another, with which we give the same guarantee.

Always bear in mind in buying a Parrot, to get it from a reliable dealer. An unhealthy, vicious bird can be doctored up by means of drugs, so as to be seemingly healthy and tame for a little while, only to relapse into a state of chronic helplessness or extreme irritability after the effects of the stimulants have passed off. It is always better to pay a few dollars more than to run the risk of getting such a bird; and thousands of such are yearly palmed-off on the unwary purchaser.

PARROTS.

The docility of Parrots, the facility with which they become accustomed to cage life, and their talent for imitating the human voice, have made them the favorite cagebird from time immemorial. No other birds become so entirely domesticated, and so much attached to their keeper; and none are so long-lived. The male and female are alike in color, and both possess the imitative faculty.

Everybody who wants to buy a Parrot desires one that talks; but such birds are not always to be had, and the prices asked for them are usually very high. It is always more satisfactory to buy a young bird and teach it yourself; which can easily be done by carrying out the instructions that here follow.

The best way to win the affection of a Parrot, is to treat it with gentleness. Approach her with harsh voice and threatening gestures, and she will immediately stand on the defensive. Approach her with soft words and kind looks, and, if not at once subdued, she will be ready to listen to what you say, and watch what you are doing. You may depend upon it, the first few interviews will be lasting, whichever way they tend. As a rule, a Parrot will learn quicker from women than men, and quicker still from children.

The best way to teach the bird to speak, is to keep quite out of sight while giving the lesson. We know of nearly a dozen parrots, of various sorts, that have been educated on this principle; and which, in a marvelously short time, have turned out fluent talkers. Too much attention cannot be paid to the linking together of words forming any sentence you may wish the bird to learn. Let each word glide into the next as smoothly as possible. If you find that your bird experiences great difficulty in repeating a particular lesson, it is better not to persist in teaching it at that time, as you may make her sullen or vicious. Before attempting to teach a Parrot to talk, it is always advisable to accustom her to being handled. The cruel plan of splitting the bird's tongue will not enable it to talk any sooner, but, on the contrary, will prevent it from ever articulating distinctly.

All species of Parrots, if fed as follows, will always keep

healthy, and a bird, to be a good talker, must always be in good condition.

In one cup of the cage always keep a mixture of dried sweet corn and canary seed; in the other, a mash, made as follows: Take a slice of stale bread, and cover it with warm water; after it has soaked for a quarter of an hour, squeeze it as dry as possible; then pour enough of boiling milk over it to moisten it without making it sloppy. This must be made fresh every day, and a tablespoonful of our Parrot Food mixed into the day's allowance. This food is made of spices, dried fruits, etc., and will keep a Parrot in brilliant plumage and health for years, if used as above directed. Price, 15c. per box; if sent by mail, 25c.

A Parrot does not need but an occasional drink of water, if fed upon moist food. Occasionally you may give them nuts of any kind (especially peanuts), boiled corn, and almost any sort of fruit. But do not feed on bread and coffee, table scraps, or meat of any kind. They have a great relish for the latter kind of food, and after awhile will acquire so determined an appetite for it, that they will pluck out their own feathers for the sole purpose of sucking the stem.

It should always be borne in mind that the gizzard of a Parrot, as well as of all other birds, takes the place of teeth; and, further, that it can no more work unless supplied with gravel than a mill can grind without millstones. Clean gravel, white or red, should be supplied, not less than three times a week.

DISEASES OF PARROTS.

In summer it is well to scald out the cup for soft food each day, and in winter at least once a week. Looseness of the bowels is the most common and dangerous ill that parrot-flesh is heir to, and nothing causes it sooner than sour food. Avoid zinc food-vessels, they are dangerous.

A Parrot should be carefully placed in the sunniest nook, and scrupulously secured from cold draughts; but these unfortunate natives of the hottest countries of the world are too often left hanging before open windows on chilly nights, and placed before chinks and crevices, through which there is sufficient draft to turn a windmill. The best treatment goes for nothing, unless a Parrot is kept warm in chilly weather.

Insufficient attention to cleanliness will cause sore feet. A Parrot's perch should be movable; and scraped and scalded at least once a week. The feet should be cleansed, when dirty, with a piece of flannel and castile soap. Parrots are sometimes attacked by a disease that seems much the same as gout with us. The feet and legs swell, and the bird is unable to grasp its perch properly. The best remedy is, to place the cage in a tub of warm water, and making her stand up to her thighs fifteen minutes, and then wipe them dry; and keep her the rest of the day before a pretty hot fire. If there are sores on the feet, apply a little sugar to them. Mix a teaspoonful of Bird Bitters in the soft food daily.

Sore eyes may proceed from cold or improper food. When the rims are red and inflamed, bathe them with a warm decoction of white hellebore. It is deadly poison, so be careful that the bird does not drink it.

Some Parrots are subject to fits. They will tumble off their perches, and, after a few convulsive struggles, lie as if dead. When this happens, squirt the coldest water you can get, over her head. If she does not revive, take her by the legs, and dip her three or four times into cold water. If she should still remain insensible, pluck out a tail feather, or cut one of her claws so as to cause it to bleed. If she does not then recover, you have a choice of two things: to have her buried or stuffed. Nothing is so likely to produce fits as costiveness, and you may know when a bird is so afflicted by her constant efforts to evacuate. For this, give three drops of castor-oil. It is no easy matter to administer castor-oil to a full-grown and strong-beaked Parrot, unless you know how. The proper way is to have a piece of hard wood, about a quarter of an inch thick and three-quarters of an inch wide; in the centre bore a hole. Open the Parrot's beak, slip in the wood, and put a quill or a glass tube through the hole, and then drop the castor-oil into the tube.

The plucking out of the feathers is nearly always caused by indulgence in animal food, or too much hemp seed. The best thing to do is to bathe the bare places with a decoction of diluted ox-gall, and diet the birds on plain canary seed, and put a teaspoonful of Bird Bitters, daily, in the soft food.

Impure water, stale food, or want of sand, will produce surfeit. The head, and sometimes the back, becomes covered with angry sores, which discharge a humor of so acrid a character that wherever it runs it removes the feathers. Dissolve a quarter of a pound of salt or half a pound of loaf sugar in a quart of water, and bathe the parts affected twice a day. Dry the sores thoroughly, and anoint them with olive oil. The diet should be as simple as possible. Boiled rice, containing a teaspoonful of Parrot Food and half a teaspoonful of Bird Bitters, is the best food, while the surfeit continues, and nothing else should be given. Keep the bird warm.

The want of proper warmth will sometimes produce inflammation. The symptoms are, melancholy, and a disposition to go to roost while it is yet daylight. If you blow up the feathers of the belly, you will find the extreme parts much swollen, and a multitude of tiny red veins showing through the skin. This is a dangerous malady, and should be seen to in time. If the bird's bowels are relaxed, give him, until better, as much magnesia as can be piled on a nickel, mixed in his soft food. A piece of sugar cane is most excellent for this disease. Feed on Parrot Food on which plenty of maw seed has been sprinkled.

The most healthy birds will sometimes be troubled with ugly wart-like excrescences. Occasionally they will grow as large as a pigeon's egg. Pass a piece of fine silk cord around the base of the tumor, and at each end of the cord make a loop; secure the cord around the excrescence by passing a small wooden peg through the loops; every other morning give the peg a twist, so as to draw the cord a little tighter, and in a short time the tumor will wither and fall off. Providing you manage the tightening of the cord with care, the operation will be attended with little or no pain. It will, however, be a long time—indeed, not till the next moult—before the bald place caused by the tumor, will be covered with feathers.

During the moulting period, Parrots require great care and attention. Sometimes considerable pain and difficulty attend the operation, and two or even three months will be thus miserably passed by the poor bird. The only way in which you can aid him is by giving him extra nourishment, and keeping him as warm as possible. It is a good plan to cover the cage entirely with brown paper. Add plenty of Parrot Food to the soft food, and a teaspoonful of Bird Bitters, daily. A biscuit (without seeds) soaked in milk, in which a few pepper pods have been boiled, is a good thing to give occasionally.

Scouring is caused either by a sudden change of diet or through taking sour fruit, or some other improper food. The symptoms are a drooping tail, a tenacious white excrement adhering to the feathers beneath the tail, and a general uneasiness exhibited by the bird. The hinder parts, which will be found to be much inflamed, should be anointed with palm-oil; give maw seed and a pepper pod, and put Bird Bitters in the soft food.

Another of the diseases to which Parrots are subject, is asthma. This either arises from an undue allowance of heating food, or through cold. The symptoms are shortness of breath, and a frequent disposition of the bird to gape. If the attack is but slight, it may be cured by altering the diet, taking care that a good portion of his food is of a moist and warm character. If the bird is very ill, make a stiff paste of boiling milk and wheat flour, and add a tablespoonful of Parrot Food, and a teaspoonful of Bird Bitters. Give him nothing else for at least three days.

THE MARICABO PARROT.

This species resembles a Double Yellow Head Mexican Parrot in color and markings, but it is smaller in size, being no larger than the Cuban. They make excellent talkers and learn very readily. The price for a good specimen is from $10.00 to $15.00.

THE BLUE ROCK PARROT.

This is a large, all-green bird, being the largest of true Parrots. They make good talkers, and are preferred by some experienced persons to the Double Yellow Head Mexican. The price for a good specimen of the Blue Rock Parrot, is from $12.00 to $20.00.

THE MACAW.

This is the largest of the Parrot family, and some kinds attain the immense size of three feet. They are among the most gaudily plumaged of birds; the variety most common being of a brilliant blue and yellow.

The upper part of this species is of a fine blue, more or less tinted with green, while the lower part from the breast downwards is a light orange yellow. The bill is entirely black, being large and strong and considerably hooked in shape. Macaws can be readily distinguished from the rest of the Parrot tribe, by the face being entirely bald, or at most furnished with a few spare lines of feathers.

The Macaw should always be chained to a perch, as in a cage its plumage is likely to be broken and injured. The perch should be strongly made, and all parts within reach of the Macaw's powerful beak, covered with tin or thin sheet brass, as a wooden perch will be destroyed by a mischievous bird in a few hours. We will furnish a suitable perch with chain for attaching to the bird's foot for $6.00. In summer the bird can be kept out of doors all the time, a roof being hung over it to protect the bird from the rain.

If bought when young, this showy bird can sometimes be taught to repeat words and sentences; but if older, it is a hopeless task to get it to utter anything except its own hideous shriek.

The diet should be coarse, and consist mainly of corn and crackers. It is very fond of nuts, the hardest of which are readily cracked by its iron-like bill.

A young male Macaw is worth from $15.00 to $50.00.

THE YELLOW-HEAD MEXICAN PARROT.

In the United States this species is, without doubt, the most popular of Parrots, and is the most fluent talker and the most easily taught. In our opinion the Mexican Parrot is the best talking bird in existence, and should be ranked even before the Gray Parrot. They are larger than the Gray Parrot, and are a beautiful green in color, with bright red on the edges of the wings and tail. Some Parrots of this species are very fond of bathing and should be often indulged in this cleanly habit, and when they will not bathe of their own free will, expose to a warm shower in summer or a bath applied by a garden syringe. There are two kinds, the DOUBLE YELLOW head and the SINGLE YELLOW head; the former being the better bird of the two, and a healthy young specimen of which is worth $12.00 to $25.00. A Single Yellow Head is worth $10.00 to $18.00. These are the prices for bright, active birds.

Talking birds of either of these varieties are worth from $25.00, up to the most fabulous prices. We know of one Mexican Parrot of the Double Yellow kind that can sing portions of over a dozen popular songs, and there is hardly a day passes that she does not add some word or sentence to her already large vocabulary. Five hundred dollars have been offered and refused for this wonderful bird.

Never teach a young Parrot the silly phrases "Pretty Polly;" "Polly wants a cracker," etc., but rather call your bird by some other name than Polly, and learn it something less stale, flat, and unprofitable than such nonsense.

THE CUBAN PARROT.

These Parrots are brought here in vast quantities every year from Cuba; and, although rather small birds, they make most excellent talkers, and learn very readily. They are green in plumage, with markings of black; and have a face of rose, edged with white. They require a rather small cage, and the treatment they need differs in no way from the general rules laid down previously. A good specimen, in the Fall, is worth $5.00; and the price advances towards Christmas to $8.00.

THE TRINIDAD PARROT resembles the above in color and size, but has not the rose face; the price is the same.

THE GRAY PARROT.

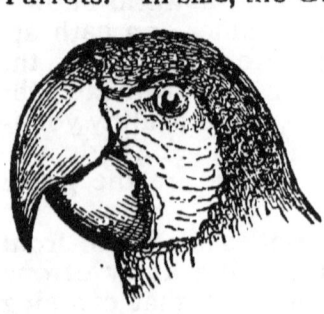

This bird, both on account of its docility, when tamed, and its superior intelligence, is among the foremost of the Parrots. In size, the Gray Parrot varies from nine to twelve inches in length. Its bill is black, strong, and much hooked, and the orbits and space between is covered with a bald white skin. The entire body is of a pearl gray, and the tail of a deep bright scarlet. When properly treated, it is one of the most healthy and longest-lived of Parrots. It makes a most excellent whistler, and will readily pick up taking airs that are repeatedly whistled to it. Never give a Gray Parrot water to drink, as it requires none, except such as is in the soft food prescribed.

A healthy young bird is worth from $12.00 to $18.00. In buying a Gray Parrot, be careful not to get one that has been brought from Liverpool on a steamer. These birds are always stowed in an unventilated box and kept in the engine-room, where they get impregnated with smoke and soot; and blood poisoning thus contracted, soon carries them off, even if seemingly healthy when bought. The healthy birds are brought on sailing vessels direct from Africa to this country.

We illustrate a stylish cage for a Gray Parrot. It is made of solid brass throughout, and has horizontal instead of vertical bars. The swing and perches are of hard wood, and the feed cups are enameled. Price, $9.00.

THE COCKATOO.

These curious members of the Parrot family are easily tamed, and although they rarely make good talkers, they become very affectionate towards their keeper. The most common of the species, the Sulphur Crested Cockatoo, is a splendid bird. The plumage is snowy white, with a tinge of lemon on the feathery crown that surmounts the head, and which he can expand at pleasure. The longest feathers of the crest measures about seven inches. He should be kept on a perch and treated as directed for Parrots. The price of a good specimen of Cockatoo, ranges from $15.00 to $30.00.

THE ROSE-BREASTED COCKATOO is no larger than a Gray Parrot. The back and tail is of a soft dove color, while the breast and crest are of a beautiful rose. They often make most excellent talkers and are very affectionate when thoroughly tamed. They should be kept in an ordinary parrot cage, and require a diet of canary seed and the soft food described under the general management of Parrots. The price ranges from $6.00 to $15.00.

THE BLUE MOUNTAIN LORY.

The Lory is of slighter build than other Parrots. The beak is more oval and slender and is prolonged before coming to a point.
THE BLUE MOUNTAIN LORY is the variety most commonly met with. His size is about that of a Pigeon and the plumage is most gorgeous, being commingled blue, scarlet, purple, and yellow. He will, if patiently taught, learn to articulate words and even sentences. Feed him on plain canary seed, and occasionally ripe fruits of any kind. The price of a good specimen is $13.00.

A suitable cage for the Blue Mountain Lory, in solid brass, is worth $6.00.

THE KING LORY.

This is the most beautiful of the Lory family and has a resplendent plumage of deep cardinal and bright green.— Their wonderful beauty is the only quality that recommends them as cage pets, as they seldom can be taught to talk and never become quite so tame as the Blue Mountain Lory.

The same diet and general treatment is required as for other members of the Lory family, but they are rather more delicate than the preceding variety and care should be taken that the cage is not hung in a draft of air or where it is cold. A small sized Parrot cage is required, the bottom of which should be daily strewn with coarse gravel.

A good specimen is worth $15.

THE BLUE HEAD AMAZON PARROT.

This variety resembles the Yellow Head Parrot in everything excepting the head, which is blue and yellow, instead of all yellow. It is also somewhat smaller. The same sort of a cage or stand is required as for other Parrots of similar size. They are quite hardy, not subject to disease, and make excellent talkers. They soon become very familiar with the person who feeds them, and will allow themselves to be handled. They are more apt to attach themselves to one person and often will not allow other members of the family to approach them.

Young Parrots of this variety will be sold under the guarantee of their talking inside of ninety days. They are worth from $8.co to $15.00 each.

BIRD FOOD CO'S PREPARATIONS FOR PARROTS.

Parrot Food, in boxes.........	15 cents,	by mail 25 cents.
" Seed, "	12 "	" " " 20 "
Red Gravel, pints............. .	5 "	" " " 35 "
Bird Bitters, per bottle,......	25 "	by mail same price.
Mexican Salve, per box......	25 "	" " " " "

BIRD CAGES, ETC.

As we keep several hundred different styles or bird cages it is impossible in this little book to describe only a few of those most popular. We deal only in the best makes and do not handle the cheaply gotten-up cages that tarnish and fall to pieces after a few months u e. Such persons as cannot make a satifactory selection from the ones illustrated in this book, can by sending ten cents have our large illustrated catalogue of cages mailed to them.

MOCKING BIRD CAGES.

Made of black walnut with tinned wire. Food cups are 25 cents per pair, extra; 20 inches long, $1.75; 22 inches long, $2.00; 24 inches long, $2.50; 26 inches long, $2.75; 28 inches long, $3.00 30 inches long, $3.50. The last two sizes with twined posts, $4.00 and $5.00 each.

CAGES FOR RED BIRDS.

Same style as for mocking birds but with seed box, 20 inches long, $2.00; 22 inches long, $2.25; 24 inches long, $2.50.

BRASS CAGES.

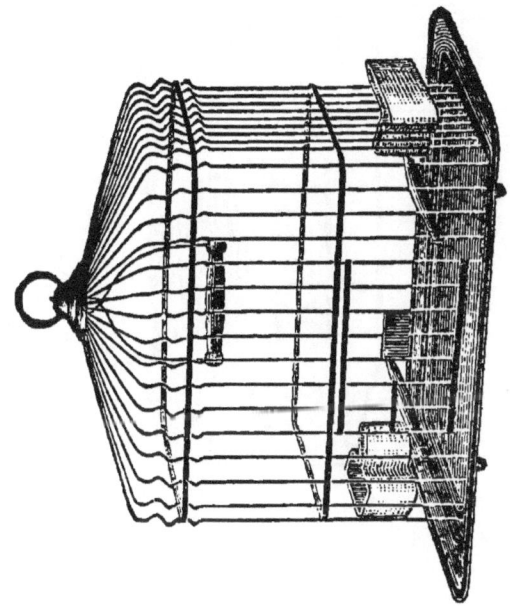

No. H 5000.
Body, 8¼ x 5 inches.
Base, 11½ x 8 inches.
Height, 10¼ inches.

Price - - - - 75 cents.

H 202. 8 inch diam. Price $1.50.
Base, 11¼ in. diam. Height, 17¼ in.

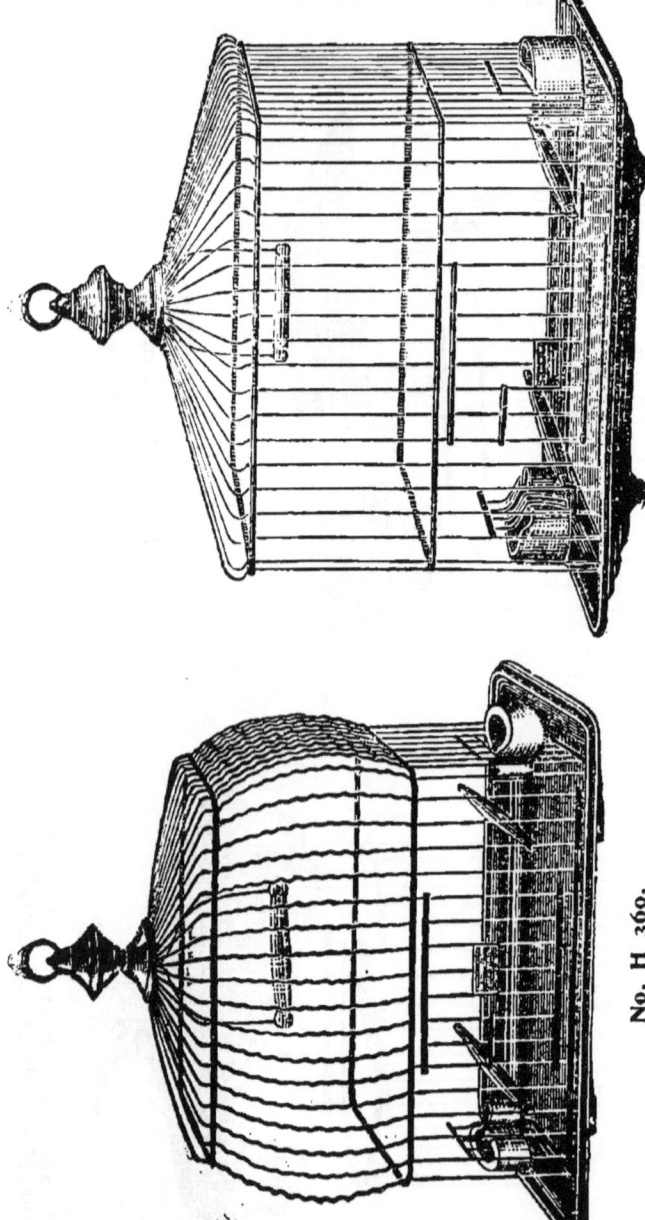

No. H 360.
Oblong Square.
Body 10½ x 8½ inches.
Base 13¼ x 11¼ inches.
Height 16½ inches.
Price $2.60. With Removable Mat, $2.75.

No. H 301.
Oblong Square. Cups and Metal Tipped Perches.
Body 10½ x 8½ inches.
Base 13¼ x 11¼ inches.
Height 14 inches.
Price $2.10. With Patent Removable Mat, $2.25.

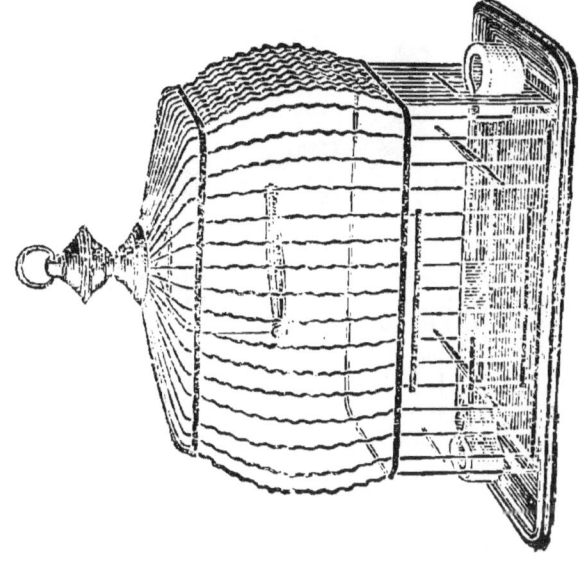

No. H 355.
Oblong Square,
Body 9½ x 7 inches.
Base 12½ x 10 inches.
Height 14½ inches.
Price $2.00.   With Removable Mat, $2.15

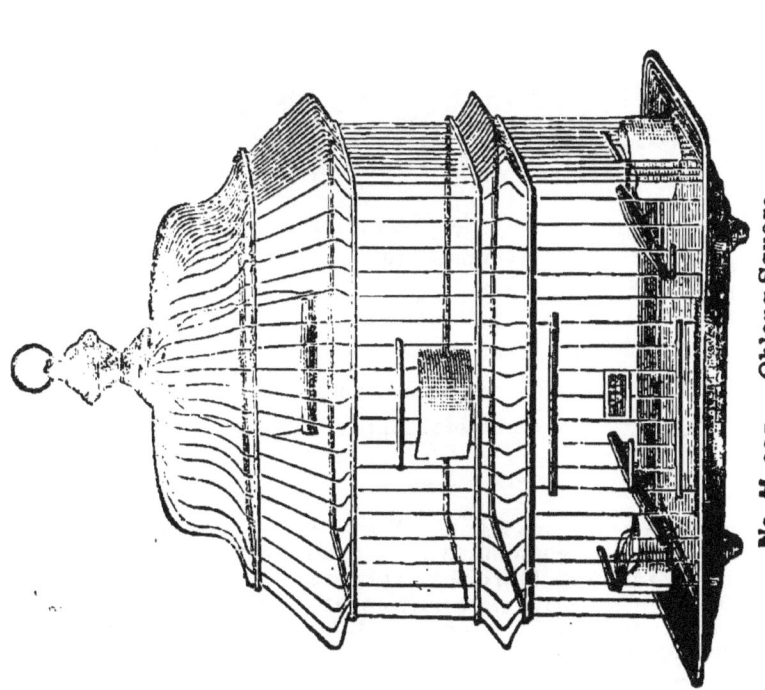

No. H 305.   Oblong Square.
Body 10¾ x 8½ inches.   Base 13¾ x 11¼ inches.
Height 18 in. $3.50.   With Removable Mat, $3.65.

No. H 345.
Oblong Square.

Body	13 x 8½ inches.
Base	15¼ x 11½ inches.
Height	19 inches.

Price $3.50. With Patent Removable Mat, $3.60.
Cups and Metal Tipped Perches.

ALBEREEN POLISHING BALLS.—For cleaning brass and metal of all kinds. They are unequalled among all cleansing preparations. They quickly remove all tarnish; oxidation and discoloration from silver, brass, nickel, plate glass mirrors, etc. The work can be safely and quickly done in half the the usual time. Price 10 cents per ball. Same price by mail.

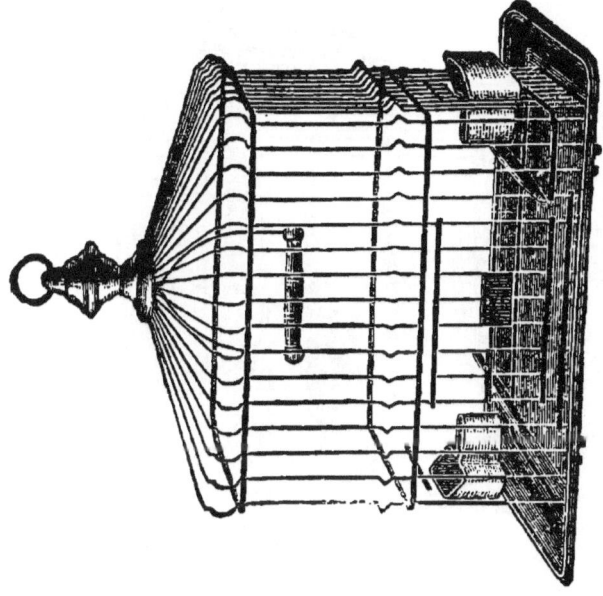

No. H 370.

Oblong Square.

Body 10¾ x 8½ inches.
Base 13 x 11¼ inches.
Height 15½ inches.

Price - - - - - - $2.75.

No. H 915.

Fancy Oblong Square.
Body 9⅝ x 7⅞ inches.
Base 12½ x 10 inches.
Height 12½ inches.

Price $2.00. With Removable Mat, $2.15.

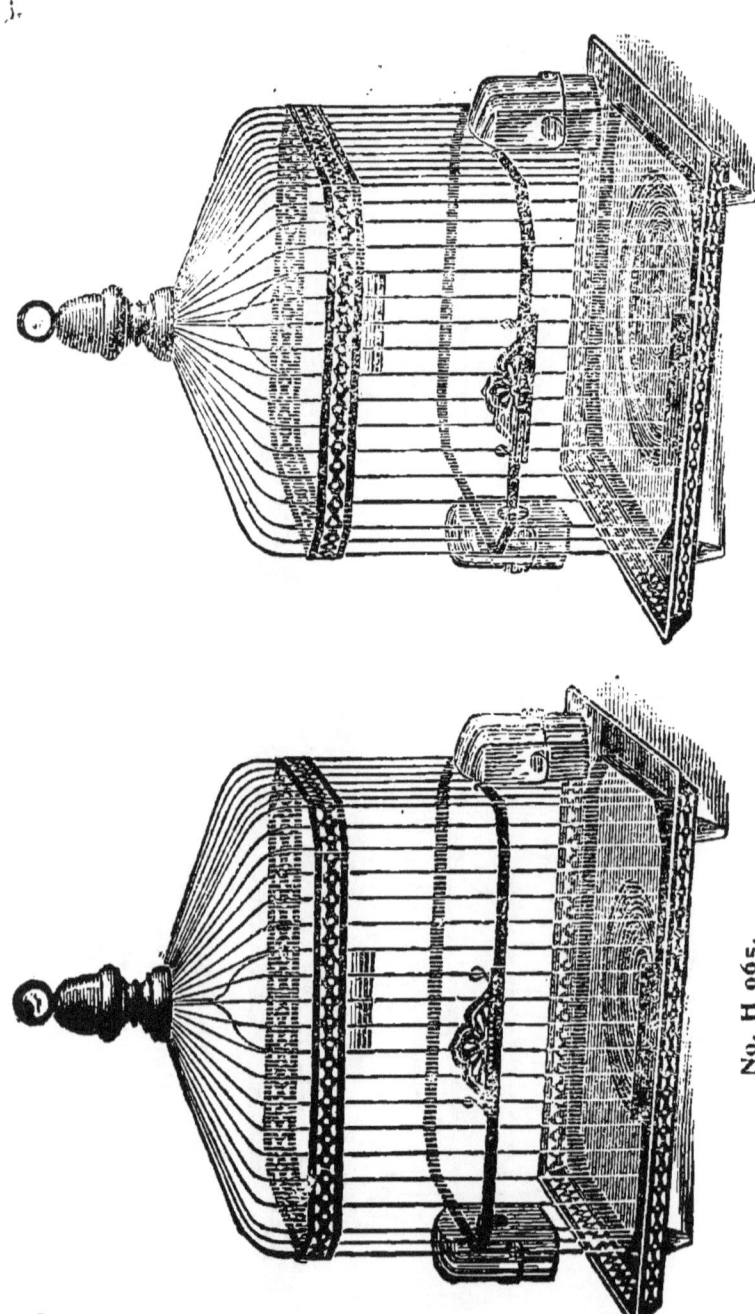

No. H 065.
New Style. Special Japanned. Fancy Oblong Square.
9¾ x 6½ inches. Height, 15½ inches.
Price 75 cts.

No. H 059.
New Style. Special Japanned. Fancy Square.
7½ x 7½ inches. Height 15 inches. Price 70 cts.

MOCKING BIRD AND BREEDING CAGES.

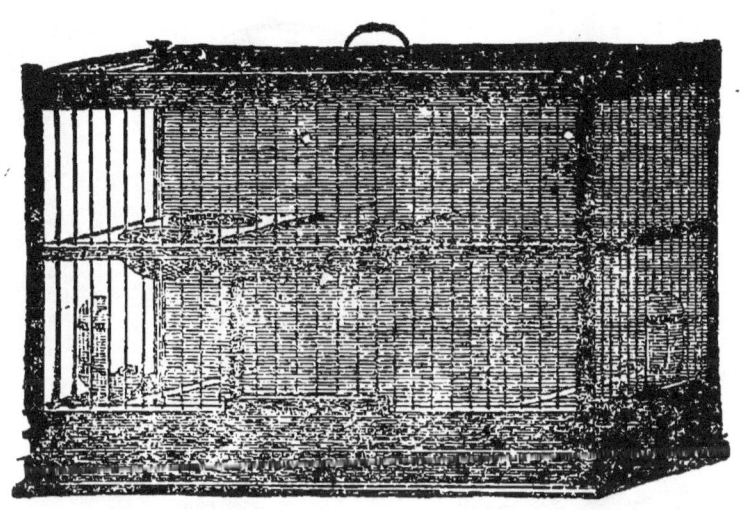

BREEDING CAGES. Tinned Wire. Walnut Frame. Zinc Drawer.

No. 1. 12x18 inches............. $1.25 each.
       12x20 " .... 1.75 "
       13x22 " .... 2.25 "
       13x24 " .... 2.75 "

Fixtures for the above cages, complete, 25 cents extra.

MOCKING BIRD CAGES.

No. 1, Length. 25½ in., Width, 15 in., Height, 24 in. Price, $3.67.
No. 2,   "   23½ "   " 13½ "   " 22½ "   "   3.20.
Extra large "   30   "   " 17½ "   "   26   "   "   4.60

CAGE FIXTURES.

All Cage Fixtures by mail, each 5 cents extra.

Climax Cups.
Opal Glass, with
Brass Tops.
Price 10 cents.

Opal Gild Band Cups.
Price 10 cents.

Glass Feed Bottles
for Wood Cages.
Price 10 cts.

Opal Crown Cups.
Price 10 cents.

Bird Baths.
China (two in a nest.) 8 cts.

Willow Birds' Nests, 10 cents.
Wire Birds' Nests, 10 cents.

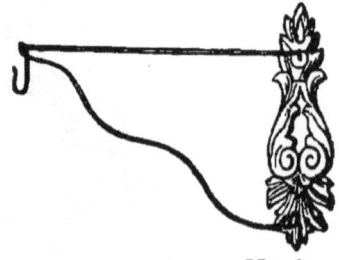

Cage Brackets. No. 1,
Price 10 cents.

No. 0, Japanned.   10 cts.
No. 00. Maroon Finish, 15 cts.

No. 1½, Maroon, Price 15 cts.

No. 11, All Solid Brass Bracket, Polished plate.   Price 50 cents.

Cage Bracket No. 2.   Price 15 cents.

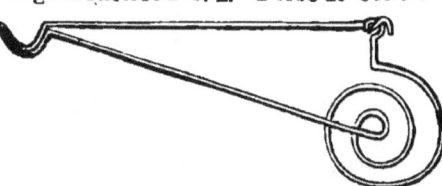

ALL WIRE CAGE BRACKETS.
No. 12.   The cheapest Bracket in the Market.   Price 5 cents.

BRIGHT TIN SQUIRREL CAGES.

Wire Front, wheel outside.

No. 1, for Chipmunks.	Wheel 6 in. diameter,	$2.25.
No. 2, for Red Squirrel.	Wheel 7½ inches, -	$2.50.
No. 3, for Gray Squirrel.	Wheel 9½ inches, -	$3.00.
No. 4, for Gray Squirrel.	Wheel 10½ inches, -	$3.50.

INDEX.

African Finches, ... 64-68
African Love Birds 94
African Parrot 102
Amazon Parrot 105
American Blue Jay 78
American Goldfinch 46
American Robin 86
American Thrush 87
Australian Parrakeet 92
Avadavat 65
Aviary Cages 23
Baltimore Oriole 82
Black-Cap 74
Black-Headed Nun 66
Blue Bird 85
Blue head Parrot 105
Blue Jay 78
Blue Mountain Lory 104
Blue Robin 85
Blue Rock Parrot 99
Bobolink 55
Brazilian Cardinal 57
Bullfinch 50
Canaries 27-44
    American-Bred. 40
    Belgian 42
    Breeding 28
    Breeding for profit 33
    Breeding in a room uncaged 32
    Cinnamon 40
    Different Varieties 37
    French 41
    German or Song 37
    Lizard 43
    London Fancy .. 43
    Manchester Coppy 44
    Mule Birds 35
    Norwich 40
    Proper care of... 27
    Red or Cayenne 39
    Scotch Fancy ... 41
    Yorkshire 42
Cages, Etc 106-118
Cardinal Grosbeak 56
Cat-Bird 80
Cedar Bird 63
Chaffinch 52
Chestnut Finch 64
Cinder Finch 68
Ciril Finch 54
Citral Finch 63
Cockateel 93
Cockatoo 103
Corden-Bleu 67
Crow 86
Crossbill 53
Cuban Parrot 103
Cut-Throat Cockatoo 102

Cut-Throat Finch	66	Parrakeets	91-94
Diamond Sparrow	67	Parrots	94-105
Diseases of Cage Birds	13	Quail	90-91
Diseases of Parrots	95	American	91
English Blackbird,	75	California	90
English Robin	76	European	90
English Thrush	74	Quaker Love Birds	94
European Jay	79	Raven	80
Fire Finch	68	Red Bird	56
Golden Robin	82	Red Linnet	53
Goldfinch	45	Rose-Breasted Grosbeak	63
Greenfinch	47	Redstart	72
Grass Parrakeet	92	Red-Winged Blackbird	62
Gray Parrot	102	Redpoll	88
Hawfinch	58	Ring Dove	89
Hermit Thrush	57	Rose-Breasted Cockatoo	103
How we sell Parrots	94	Scarlet Tanager	88
In-Door Aviary	18	Seed-Eating Birds	9
Indigo Finch	61	Sending Birds by Express	7
Jackdaw	84	Serin Finch	54
Japanese Robin	76	Silverbeak	65
Java Sparrow	58	Siskin	49
King Lory	104	Skylark	81
Linnet	48	Soft Billed Birds	12
Lories	104	Starling	84
Love Birds	94	Stuffing Birds	26
Macaw	100	Sulphur Crested Cockatoo	103
Magpie	77		
Magpie Finch	67	Swamp Robin	85
Manakin	66	Thrasher	87
Maricabo Parrakeet	93	Titmice	59
Maricabo Parrot	99	Trapping Birds	25
Mino	77	Tropial	83
Mocking Bird	68	Waxbill	64
Mule Birds	35	Weaver Bird	61
Nestling Food	17	Whidah Bird	60
Nightingale	73	White Dove	89
Nonpareil	55	White-Headed Nun	65
Nutmeg Finch	64	Woodlark	82
Orange Cheek Waxbill	67	Yellowhammer	62
Oriole	82	Zebra Finch	65
Out-Door Aviary	21		

www.ingramcontent.com/pod-product-compliance
Lightning Source LLC
Chambersburg PA
CBHW031403160426
43196CB00007B/882